Making Good in the Ministry

Making Good in the Ministry

A Sketch of John Mark

By

PROF. A. T. ROBERTSON, M.A., D.D., LL.D.

Professor of New Testament Interpretation,
Southern Baptist Theological Seminary,
Louisville, Ky.

BROADMAN PRESS
NASHVILLE, TENNESSEE

Paperback edition issued by
Broadman Press
First printing, January 1976
ISBN: 0-8054-1516-5 (complete set)
4215-16
0-8054-1513-0 (this volume)
4215-13

To

MY STUDENTS

Preface

WITH May, 1918, I complete thirty years as a teacher of young preachers. About four thousand during this period have been my pupils besides hundreds of young women. They are scattered all over the world as workers for Christ and some have gone on before. My own life will count for much or little in proportion as these men and women do well the work that God has placed in their hands. I love them with my whole heart and this, my twentieth book, alas, deals directly with the failure or success of one's life-work as illustrated by John Mark. My very heart has gone into this book and with it a message to all workers for Christ, young and old, all over the world of whatever creed. John Mark has a message for us all. It is not easy to-day to make a success of one's ministry. It never was easy. It never will be easy. Ministerial fidelity makes success possible. There is something sweeter than success. It is to deserve it.

A. T. R.

Louisville, Ky.

Contents

I

THE HOME ATMOSPHERE

"He came to the house of Mary the mother of John whose surname was Mark; where many were gathered together and were praying."

—ACTS 12:12.

I

THE HOME ATMOSPHERE

1. The Home that Makes Preachers.

IT is in the home that, as a rule, preachers are made or unmade. Instance Scotland where in the palace of the laird or in the thatch-roofed cottage of the cottar the mother wishes no higher crown for her boy than that he be "a good minister of Christ Jesus" and live to "speak a gude word for Jesus." In many so-called Christian homes to-day it would be considered a positive misfortune if the sons heeded the call of God to become preacher, missionary, or Y. M. C. A. worker or if the girls likewise responded to the voice of duty which is the voice of God. It must be confessed that some homes are a positive hindrance to the young lives that throb in response to the clamoring calls of to-day, who, like Joan of Arc, hear voices calling them out and on to China, to India, to Brazil. The Student

Volunteer Movement has brought definite decision to thousands who had hitherto dodged the great question of a life calling and had drifted on with smothered conscience. The Y. M. C. A. and Y. W. C. A. summer conferences have likewise proved to be the hour of destiny for many more who had not found their Bethel at home, in church, or in college. But the home has the first chance at the boy. He can never quite get over the nesting-place and ought not to have to forget it. The difficulty in finding workers for various forms of Christian activity to-day is at bottom the problem of the home.

2. **A City Home.**

John Mark lived in the city and not in the country. To-day nearly all the recruits for active Christian service come from the country homes. Young men in the city can hear the call of country, but not so readily the call of God. City youths have to respond under a universal draft law, but they showed up well under the volunteer system in comparison with the country young men. But the din of the city drowns the still small voice of

God. The clamor of the market crowds out the appeal of the Spirit. The clink of gold clutches at the heart that ought to be sensitive to the presence of the Man Christ Jesus. So we look to the hills for the preachers, for nature there allows some opportunity for the things of the spirit to have a hearing. At least it did before the telephone, the automobile, the interurban car, and the parcel post came to the country. What these material comforts will yet do to the spiritual life in the country home and the country church remains to be seen. Already the country church is in dire peril, we are told.

But Christ can dwell in hearts that live in city homes and young preachers can come out of this city atmosphere. In the first century A. D. it was, as a rule, dangerous to live in the country. People who toiled in the country lived in villages and towns as in China now. The city ruled the ancient world as it is coming to do in America. We must not admit that city homes have no obligations to God in the matter of ministerial supply. The balance of population will soon be in favor of the city in the United States.

It is hard to turn the heart to the service of Christ in an atmosphere dominated by the moving picture shows or by the mad rush for money, place, or power. But Christ won a hearing even in Jerusalem, held, as it was, in the grip of tradition, where scribe and priest shut the door in the face of those who wished to learn and threw away the key to knowledge. But they crucified Christ in the end. The first thing to note about John Mark is that he lived in the city.

3. **A Home of Some Wealth.**

The city, alas, has homes and homes. The tenement house is almost a hell unless Christ has come into the heart of the owner and He makes it a model tenement hall. Even the palatial apartment houses are not very homelike and the great hotels have no home atmosphere at all. Better far a cottage with Christ than a palace without Him, grand and cheerless and chill. But Christ will enter the palace if the owner gives Him the key to his heart and makes room for Him there. Mary's house was a home of wealth. Mark was a cousin[1] of Barnabas (Col. 4:10). Bar-

[1] So ἀνεψιός is to be rendered, not "sister's son."

nabas was a man of means and of great generosity (Acts 4:36 f.). As he was a Levite and from Cyprus, the family of Mark probably came from that island. The house of Mary had a gate and a passageway leading to the inner court, "the door of the gate,"[1] somewhat like a Scotch "close." The door was next to the street (Luke 13:25). There was a gateway or passageway to the house of Simon the Tanner in Joppa (Acts 10:17). In New Orleans to-day the old French houses have an inner court which is entered by an outside gate. The house of Mary was large enough for a considerable company, "many" (Acts 12:12), to be gathered. The presence of the slave-girl or doorkeeper is another indication of a well-to-do home as in the house of Caiaphas (John 18:16). "Mary's house," therefore, had been a place of importance in the social life of Jerusalem before she became a Christian. She then made it a center of Christian activity as Martha and Mary had made their Bethany home, likewise a home of ease and some affluence, the home of Jesus

[1] Acts 12:13 τὴν θύραν του πυλῶνος. In Matthew 26:71 τὸν πυλῶνα is "the porch." The fact of a "porch" shows that it was a house of some size.

(Luke 10:38–42). There was thus "a church in Mary's house" in Jerusalem as in that of Prisca and Aquila in Rome (Rom. 16:5) and of Philemon (Philemon 2) and of Nymphas in Colossæ (Col. 4:15). The house was spacious and gave the Christians a place to meet when they could no longer assemble in temple or synagogue in Jerusalem as was now the case. Peter himself was just out of prison and fear gripped again the community of believers in the city. It is thought by some that "the upper room" (Acts 1:13) where the disciples met for prayer when they were waiting for the promise of the Father was in Mary's house. Some even hold[1] that it was in Mary's house that Jesus observed the last passover meal and instituted the supper (Mark 14:12–25). But it is at least clear that John Mark lived in a home of comparative ease and of good social standing.

4. A Home Where Christ is King.

This is what matters most. Wealth, culture, social leadership, power, all should be laid at the feet of Jesus. Mary had taken

[1] Cf. Edersheim, "Life and Times of Jesus the Messiah," Vol. II, p. 485.

her stand uncompromisingly for Christ her Lord. She had thus broken away from the strong Jewish environment of her Levite kinspeople. She was helped, to be sure, by Barnabas, her kinsman, and, being probably a Hellenistic Jew, she was not quite so closed to new ideas as the average Palestinian Jew. The tyranny of one's social class is merciless, as many a woman discovers who cuts through it all and comes out into actual and active service for Christ. She is termed peculiar and unfashionable and runs the risk of the social taboo. But Mary threw her beautiful home wide open to Christ instead of to the world. There are such homes to-day in our modern cities, homes of great wealth, the highest culture, the truest aristocracy, the most genuine piety. Such a home is not made without a fight against worldliness with all its insidious allurements. Jesus astonished the disciples exceedingly by saying: "It is easier for a camel to go through a needle's eye, than for a rich man to enter the Kingdom of God" (Mark 10:25). "Then who can be saved?" they asked, feeling that it was easier for the rich than for the poor. Jesus meant to state a natural impossibility:

"With men it is impossible, but not with God: for all things are possible with God" (Mark 10:27). Thank God both rich and poor can enter the Kingdom of God and on precisely the same terms, full surrender and simple trust. Service flags and Red Cross flags hang in the windows of many homes to-day because of loyalty to our country. Christ is King. Let Him be Lord of our homes and of all the home life, openly and aboveboard, so that all the world may know where our loyalty lies.

5. The Widowed Mother.

"Evidently a widow," Ramsay[1] says, since there is no mention of the husband and father and since it is "the house of Mary." She was "another Mary, another of those women whose praise was in the early church."[2] The other "Marys" were the mother of Jesus, the wife of Cleopas, the mother of James and Joses, Mary Magdalene, and Mary of Bethany. The name was common with the Jews because of Miriam, the

[1] "Pictures of the Apostolic Church," 1910, p. 109.

[2] Rackham, "The Acts of the Apostles," 1909, p. 178.

sister of Moses. Luke pictures this Mary from the standpoint of the later development as "the mother of John whose surname was Mark." She came to live in the reflected glory of her noble son after he rose to usefulness and fame. This was as she wished it to be, as any true mother would have it. But at this stage of the history Mark was simply Mary's son with his future before him with all its problems, hopes, and fears. Mary is the queen of this home and her spirit reigned within its walls. She created the atmosphere which all breathed who entered her home. It was the aroma of a lofty soul who lived with Christ and loved to bless all around her with the grace and charm of her rich character. Mary was a leader in the church by force of Christian character and the dynamic of love that made her unwilling to be a negative quantity in the life of the Jerusalem church. She had initiative and resource and courage. She was not afraid to open her home to the disciples at the very time when their leader, Simon Peter, was in prison and when James, the brother of John, had been beheaded by Herod Agrippa to please the Jews (Acts 12:1 f.). Her courage was contagious, as we can easily see, and steadied some of the wavering ones.

6. The Gathering for Prayer.

Prayer had been going on without ceasing since the arrest of Peter (Acts 12:5). Agrippa was simply waiting till the passover feast was over and the crowd was gone to have Peter put to death, strangely like the plan of the Sanhedrin about Jesus before Judas came to the rescue (Luke 22:6). The disciples knew the peril of Peter with the fate of James before their very eyes. Prison doors had opened before for Peter and John (Acts 5:19) and once before they had prayed to God for boldness to defy the ecclesiastical authorities and God had heard their cry (Acts 4:23–31). But this time it was the hand of the state that was stretched forth against them and the Christians, though now many thousands strong in Jerusalem, were still in a great minority. They seemed to have prayed night and day.[1] The exigency was great. Perhaps the disciples came and

[1] Luke's words in 12 : 5 (ἐκτενῶς γινομένη) seem to mean that, though "earnestly" is the translation. Luke uses ἐκτενέστερον of the prayer of Christ in the Garden of Gethsemane (Luke 22 : 44).

went, but the praying went on. The church's leaders seem to have been absent this night, for "James and the brethren" (12:17) had a message sent them. Whether it just happened so or the leaders were assembled elsewhere for caution we do not know. But a great crowd (probably mostly Hellenistic Christians) were on hand this night. "The supplication of a righteous man availeth much in its working" (Jas. 5:16). In prayer these disciples turned "to that alliance which is indeed invincible" (Chrysostom, *Hom.* 26). "It is an early instance of the Christian custom of spending the whole night in watching and prayer" (Rackham, "Commentary," p. 178). Jesus had set the example. Paul held an all night service at Troas (Acts 20:7–12). And there was real praying going on, we may be sure, prayer for the deliverance of Simon Peter from prison, prayer for this specific blessing.

7. Peter's Visit.

Here was the hand of God beyond a doubt. On the same night on which Agrippa had planned to bring Peter forth and kill him to add to the pleasure of the Jews (12:3, 6) God interposed and answered the prayer of the church for Peter (12 : 5) by sending an angel or messenger,[1] for the word is used both ways. But there is no way to get rid of the supernatural interposition of God in direct answer to the prayers of the disciples. It is a graphic story, the dazed stupor of Peter as he is led out, freed from his chains, past the first guard and then the second, through the iron gate that opened of its own accord, and out on the street at last, free. The angel was gone and Peter "came to himself"[2] and recognized the hand of God and his own danger. God had delivered him "out of the hand of Herod, and from all the expectations of the people of the Jews" (12 : 11), but Peter had no notion of sitting still and waiting till Herod arrested him again, for he was bound to learn of his escape as he did. So he "considered"[3] the thing and came to the house of Mary. It was probably after 3 A. M. (Furneaux, "Acts," p. 182), but he was, like the other disciples, a frequent visitor at this hospitable home and

[1] *ἄγγελος Κυρίου* (12 : 7).

[2] *ἐν ἑαυτῷ γενόμενος* (12 : 11), like Luke's phrase about the Prodigal Son *εἰς ἑαυτὸν ἐλθών* (Luke 15 : 17).

[3] *συνιδών* (cf. 14 : 6), looking at it together or as a whole.

he was sure of a welcome and of refuge for the moment. Possibly "some special tie existed between him and this family" (Furneaux, *ibid.*). He calls Mark "his son" (1 Pet. 5 : 13), and he may have been the means of winning the young man to Christ. The disciples could hear his knocking and the maid [1] went to answer [2] the knock at this strange hour of the night, though all were awake and at prayer. Rhoda (Rose) knew Peter's voice, because he was a frequent guest at the house, and knew that the company was keeping all night vigil for his release. Her conduct is drawn to the life as, through excess of joy, she left Peter standing on the outside and still in peril while she ran back and told the anxious group that Peter stood there before the gate (12 : 14). It was a moment when overwrought nerves snap. When Jesus appeared to the disciples in the upper room on the night of the Resurrection Day, they disbelieved for joy (Luke 24 : 41).

[1] παιδίσκη. Portress or slave-girl. "Domestic slaves were at that time treated generally as humble members of the family in pagan, much more in Christian, households" (Ramsay, "Pictures of the Apostolic Church," p. 109).

[2] ὑπακοῦσαι. Suggests listening before opening.

Human nature at high tension does not work by rule. So now, with the answer to their prayer at the gate, they turn on the poor girl and say, "Thou art mad." Her confident reiteration brought the interpretation that it was "his angel" (12 : 15), whether his ghost or his guardian angel, as some held to be true, is not clear. But Peter (the ghost!) kept on knocking[1] till finally the whole company ("they") hurried down the courtyard, as a protection to each other, and bravely opened the door and faced Simon Peter himself to their utter amazement. Their prayer was answered as they had really expected it to be, but it was all so sudden and it was too good to be true. Our faith is weak at best and has its own little rules for the Lord to work by. Peter, almost in terror, beckoned to the excited throng to be still, told his story, bade them tell "James and the brethren," and "went to another place" (12 : 17) before he could be found by Herod Agrippa. He may have gone on to Antioch or to Rome. James, the Lord's brother, is already the leader in Jerusalem.

[1] ἐπέμενεν κρούων (12 : 15). Imperfect tense and supplementary participle.

8. **And Young John Mark.**

He was an interested spectator of the events of this night. Ramsay[1] thinks that Rhoda told Luke this vivid story, for she alone knew all the details. Perhaps so, but John Mark could have also told Luke.[2] There was evidently much talk after Peter was gone and all the items were rehearsed, one by one. We do not know the age of John Mark at this time, but he was probably in the early twenties. Some think he was the man "bearing a pitcher of water" (Luke 22:10) who was to guide Peter and John to the house for the passover meal: "Follow him into the house whereinto he goeth." He is also held by some to be the "certain young man" of Mark 14:51 f. who followed Jesus into the Garden of Gethsemane and fled naked when the officers tried to arrest him. Papias, however, is quoted by Eusebius as saying of Mark that "he neither heard the Lord nor followed him." But almost certainly he was a Christian by the time of this incident in Acts 12.

[1] "Pictures of the Apostolic Church," p. 110.

[2] So Knowling, "Expositor's Greek Testament, Acts," p. 276.

Holdsworth[1] thinks that Mark was one of the six brethren that accompanied Peter from Joppa to Cæsarea (Acts 10 : 23). "Eusebius tells that St. Mark was sent to Egypt in the first year of the Emperor Claudius, which would be in A. D. 41, and both Eusebius and Jerome tell us that he took his Gospel with him. St. Chrysostom tells us that he wrote his Gospel in Egypt." Holdsworth is here arguing for the view that Mark wrote three editions of his Gospel, one in Cæsarea for the household of Cornelius (cf. Acts 10 : 34–43, where the same broad outline is given as in Mark's Gospel), one in Egypt, and one in Rome (our Mark). This is an interesting hypothesis, but it cannot be called a fact. We are only concerned with it here for the light that it throws on the activities of John Mark at this period. In that case we should think of him as at least thirty. It is quite possible that he had already been Peter's interpreter in his work at Joppa and Cæsarea. If so, this bond makes it plainer still why he went at once to Mary's

[1] "Gospel Origins," 1913, p. 115. Ramsay ("St. Paul the Traveller and Roman Citizen," p. 51) makes the persecution of James and Peter by Herod Agrippa in the early part of A. D. 44.

house. But, at any rate, this youth is already in touch with the leaders of the Jerusalem church. He is kin to Barnabas, is a protégé of Simon Peter, and in his mother's circle of friends, who flock to her home as a sort of Christian *salon*, he comes to know the chief spirits of the time. It is impossible to overestimate the influence for good of the presence in the home of the noble men and women whom the children there meet. Gladstone brought the great souls of his day to Hawarden Castle so that his children might come in touch with them. John Mark had this influence on his early life and it left its impress upon him. Like Saul (Paul) he had both a Jewish and a Roman name. There is no doubt at all that this "John Mark" of Acts 12:12 is the "John" of 13:5, 13 and the "Mark" of 1 Peter 5:13 and Colossians 4:10; 2 Timothy 4:11. It is possible that Mark may have been a regular "synagogue-minister,"[1] like the man in Luke 4:20, before his conversion, though the same word in Acts 13:5 used of Mark may have a more general application. If this were true, it would indicate that Mark was a man familiar with re-

[1] Technical use of ὑπηρέτης.

ligious work, with the rolls of Scripture, and something of a practical linguist as we know that he was later. He knew well both the Aramaic and the current Greek (*Koine*) and spoke both fluently so that he could act as interpreter or dragoman for a speaker like Peter. We do not know that he had as yet seriously considered becoming a preacher like Peter or Barnabas, but the question must have been forced upon his attention in this atmosphere. Who can tell what were his mother's prayers about her son? Who can tell what thoughts throb in a young man's mind and heart? Perhaps Barnabas and Peter had already asked Mark what his life-choice would be. Was God calling him into the ministry for Jesus? If that happens to a man, it usually occurs to others as well as to the man himself.

II

THE CALL OF OPPORTUNITY

"*Taking with them John whose surname was Mark.*"
—ACTS 12: 25.

II

THE CALL OF OPPORTUNITY

WE do not always know when opportunity knocks at our door. Many of the great decisions of life are made without our meaning to make them. We take a step and then another and we are off upon the great adventure of life.

1. An Incidental Trip.

It is clear that Mark went along without meaning as yet to commit himself on the great question of his life-calling. "Barnabas and Saul returned from Jerusalem, when they had fulfilled their ministration, taking with [1] them John whose surname was Mark"

[1] συνπαραλαβόντες. Taking along together with (two prepositions). This very word with both prepositions occurs again in connection with Mark in Acts 15 : 37 f. Paul uses it also (Gal. 2 : 1) about taking Titus with him to Jerusalem. The word shows that Mark was "an unofficial companion" (Ramsay, "St. Paul the Traveller," p. 177).

(Acts 12:25). Barnabas and Saul may have stopped at the home of Mary during their stay in Jerusalem. Peter and the apostles were apparently away. The absence of Peter, Mark's "chosen friend and teacher," made Mark more open to the influence of his cousin Barnabas and to the personality of Saul, a protégé of Barnabas, whom he had brought from Tarsus to Antioch to help him in the work there (Acts 11:25 f.). Probably both men had been considering Mark's useful gifts for the campaign among the Gentiles which they may already have been planning (Rackham, p. 183). "He had a good knowledge of Greek together with the faculty of composition. Moreover he was thoroughly acquainted with the teaching of Peter and the oral traditions of the church of Jerusalem" (*Ibid.*). If he had already had some experience with Peter as interpreter, so much the better. "But he had been living among the narrow prejudices of the Jerusalem church, and the sequel suggests that the relationship with Barnabas rather than his sympathy with Saul's views led him to accompany him" (Furneaux, "Acts," pp. 189 f.). So, perhaps without great stirrings of heart, Mark consented to go to Antioch. It was a pleasant enough journey and there was a chance of being of service. So he agreed to go. "This incidental notice of John Mark may well emphasize the fact that he was taken with Paul and Barnabas as a supernumerary, and to mark his secondary character as compared with them" (Knowling, "Commentary," p. 281). But Mary may well have had fluttering of heart as her son started out upon what proved to be a great expedition. Rackham ("Commentary," p. 183) thinks that the Roman "prænomen" *Marcus* was given John at this juncture with a view to its giving him some help in his travels, "like most Jews who travelled in the Græco-Roman world." But of that we do not know. At any rate Mark was willing to go with Barnabas and Saul to Antioch.[1]

2. **With Two Great Men.**

It may be that Mark was not quite aware of the spiritual greatness of the two men who invited him to be their companion to Antioch. He ought to have appreciated Barnabas, his

[1] The reading "to" (εἰς) Jerusalem is manifestly erroneous even though supported by ℵ *B*.

kinsman, though sometimes ties of blood make it harder to appraise one so near to us. Saul had not yet come to the full stature of his manhood in Christ, but his great gifts were long ago made manifest in the persecution of the Jews which he had led. The fact that Barnabas had championed Saul's cause and believed his story, when the other leaders in Jerusalem were both sceptical and afraid (Acts 9:26f.), and had himself brought Saul from Tarsus to Antioch to help him in his work, would predispose Mark to look on Saul with admiration. "The personality of Saul may have kindled the young man's enthusiasm" (Furneaux, "Acts," p. 189). There is nothing that appeals to a young man more strongly than a really great man. Hero worship comes natural to youth. Usually they know the quality of their heroes pretty well. Ramsay[1] notes the "curiously incidental way" in which "John Mark is brought before the reader's notice here" in order "to emphasize the secondary character of John Mark" "as a supernumerary and subordinate." "The silence is singularly expressive and therefore calculated" on

[1] "St. Paul the Traveller and Roman Citizen," p. 71.

Luke's part. But there was no effort on the part of Barnabas and Saul to depreciate Mark or to make him feel uncomfortable. They probably had high hopes for his future. At any rate, after delivering their alms from Antioch, "they took back in exchange some living gold—they took with them John Mark" (Rackham, "Acts," p. 183). Great preachers are constantly on the lookout for other men with the divine spark of consecration that lifts a man out of the ordinary and that makes possible the highest usefulness. Did John Mark possess the holy fire that would kindle a flame in other lives, among Greeks as well as among Jews? He had probably served his apprenticeship with Simon Peter among the Jews and the Romans. Now he was to have his chance with the Greeks.

3. In a Greek Church.

In Antioch Mark would be able to see for himself what the Holy Spirit was doing with and for the Greeks. He knew the story of the work in Jerusalem from Pentecost on. He may have seen the Roman Pentecost at Cæsarea in the house of Cornelius. At Antioch he witnessed the outpouring of the

Holy Spirit upon the Greek church "as they ministered to the Lord and fasted" (Acts 13:2). There were prophets and teachers in that church, as there ought to be in every church, men with the prophetic message and the teaching gift. Indeed, each preacher ought to combine these two functions in varying degrees. Christianity cannot well make progress without both gifts whether found in one man or in two. The prophet is needed first to set on fire the soul with holy passion, but the teacher must follow with instruction to keep the fire burning else it may burn out. No mention is made of Mark's attitude toward the great event in Antioch when the Holy Spirit made a distinct call for Barnabas and Saul to be set apart "for the work whereunto I have called them" (13:2). This was not a call to become missionaries in the sense of preaching to Gentiles, for this was a Gentile church in Antioch and both men had already entered upon that work. But it was a call to go on a great world campaign to win Gentiles to Christ. At Cæsarea and at Antioch the impulse had come from God and the work had not yet spread far and no formal program for further expansion had been proposed. Mark probably knew of the way that the Pharisaic Christians in Jerusalem had tried to discredit Peter's work in Cæsarea (Acts 11:1–18) and the skillful defense made by Peter with their reluctant acquiescence. But now a new crisis was sprung. The church at Antioch was called upon by the Holy Spirit, or at least the prophets and teachers were, to approve the new and epochal campaign among the Gentiles. They were not asked to pay for it, but to pray for it. This they did with great heartiness, for they were Greeks themselves, and that is more than the church at Jerusalem would have done with so many Pharisaic Christians in the membership and with the apostles scattered over the world. It was a stirring time. Jerusalem had tarried too long and had lost her primacy in the kingdom. The twelve apostles were still preaching to Jews, save Peter's experience at Cæsarea. The Great Commission was now to be carried out by two men not in the college of the twelve, but both apostles (missionaries) in the real sense of the word and both specifically called to this great enterprise. John Mark was inevitably moved by what he saw and heard at Antioch.

4. **Barnabas' Leadership.**

This is made plain by the call of the Holy Spirit. Barnabas is named before Saul as the head of the expedition. In the list of prophets and teachers named in the church in Antioch (Acts 13:1) Barnabas heads the list and Saul comes last. It will hardly do to say that Luke is staging his persons for dramatic effect. Saul could well recall the words of Jesus to him in Jerusalem: "Depart: for I will send thee forth far hence unto the Gentiles" (Acts 22:21). But Jesus had not said to Saul that he was to be the great apostle of the ages to the Gentiles. That belonged to the future and Saul had gladly coöperated with Barnabas in Antioch and was apparently glad enough to work under him in the new arrangement. Barnabas had been sent to Antioch by the Jerusalem church (Acts 11:22), but he had conserved the independence of the Antiochian church while preserving the utmost amity by taking alms to the relief of the Jerusalem poor (11:29 f.) at the time of the famine.

John Mark probably took his cousin's leadership as a matter of course as did the whole church at Antioch. Saul was still just the co-worker of Barnabas.

5. To Go On or to Go Back.

John Mark had not been named by the Holy Spirit in the call, but only Barnabas and Saul. The farewell meeting was evidently held in honor of Barnabas and Saul and, after fasting and prayer, hands were laid upon them, not in the technical sense of "ordination" to the ministry or for the bestowal of the Holy Spirit. Both had already received the gift of the Holy Spirit (Acts 9 : 17; 11 : 24) and both had long been active ministers. It was a sort of dedicatory service in view of the new and solemn enterprise to which they were called by the Holy Spirit. Certainly Saul, in view of the events connected with his conversion and the message of Jesus through Ananias (Acts 9 : 6, 15 f.; 22 : 14 f.) was only too willing to enter this open door. He had not been idle at Tarsus, but here at last was his real life-work. The duty of Barnabas was clear and his work at Antioch with the Greeks had the seal of

God's blessing (Acts 11 : 24–26) and the Holy Spirit's present call was explicit. He was under orders and he was ready to go. What was John Mark to do? A narrow and sensitive man might have shown irritation or even resentment at not being named in the call of the Holy Spirit. He was only "an extra hand" (Ramsay, "St. Paul the Traveller," p. 71) taken on the responsibility of Barnabas and Saul. One step at a time is the way that God leads us. Mark had come to Antioch with Barnabas and Saul. Now they were clearly led on and out into a world campaign for Christ upon a quest full of adventure and uncertainty. The very novelty of it all would appeal to a young man like Mark. Barnabas and Saul wanted him to go on with them and explained how they needed him and could make his journey useful as well as agreeable. So he agreed to go on with them. Perhaps he sent back a message to his mother Mary about this further step and asked for her approval and for her prayers. The party were sent forth by the Holy Spirit and with the best wishes of the Greek church in Antioch (Acts 13:3 f.) now become the center of one of the great world movements of all time.

III

TAKING A HUMBLE PLACE

"*And they had also John as their attendant.*"

—ACTS 13:5.

III

TAKING A HUMBLE PLACE

PRECISELY what John Mark's place in the company was we do not know, but certainly it was a subordinate one. Here was a call from man and not to a very high place. Was it also the call of God and was it worth while? Very few young ministers are placed at once upon a pinnacle and, if they are, they often become dizzy and sometimes fall. In the ministry, as in business callings, it matters far more what one does with his position than what the place is. It is far better to do a big work in a little place than a little work in a big place. It is not even certain what John had to do.

1. The Synagogue Minister?

The word[1] here translated "attendant" is

[1] *ὑπηρέτην.* Literally an under-rower with other rowers above one in the boat.

sometimes used for the official *chazzan* or synagogue minister as in Luke 4:20. The Greek idiom quite allows this translation. "The clause is in close connection with the mention of synagogues; the omission of the article is common in the case of official titles; and, if it was a predicate, the natural order of the Greek words would be different" (Furneaux, "Acts," p. 197). This is all true and makes out at least a plausible argument for this translation. The word is used also for "officers" who were sent to arrest Jesus (John 7:32, 45). The *chazzan* in the synagogue in Luke 4:20 handed the Lord Jesus the roll like a modern beadle or sexton. If this view be taken, we have another item about Mark that links him closely with Judaism. He would, as a regular synagogue minister, be very handy in the preaching services which were always held in the synagogues if allowed by the Jewish authorities. This was Paul's constant practice, as we know, except in a few cases as at Lystra (Acts 14:15). There were excellent reasons for this conduct even though Paul was the apostle to the Gentiles. He still felt that the Gospel came to the Jew first (Rom. 2:10) and, being a Jewish rabbi himself, the heathen in the public places would be prejudiced against him as toward all Jews (cf. the case of Alexander at Ephesus, Acts 19 : 34). Besides, as a rabbi, he would have access to the synagogues and there would also meet the many God-fearing Gentiles (Acts 17 : 17) who had turned to Judaism for some relief from the myths and licentiousness of current heathenism or from the still worse emperor cult. "Hence the synagogue attracted numerous proselytes, and a preacher of the Gospel found in it a bridge over which to pass to pagan circles" (Furneaux, "Acts," p. 197).

2. The Baptizer?

We know that Peter "commanded them to be baptized in the name of Jesus Christ" (Acts 10 : 48) when Cornelius and his household were converted. John Mark, as we have seen, may have been one of the six with Peter who attended to this baptizing. Paul usually had others to do the baptizing for him to keep down small jealousies on that point (1 Cor. 1 : 14–17). Blass (Acts, *in loco*) explains "attendant" or "minister" as "for baptizing" (*velut ad baptizandum*). The prophets sometimes had servants or attendants as Elisha to Elijah (1 Kings 19:21) and Gehazi to Elisha (2 Kings 4:12). It is hardly likely that John Mark came along to do simply personal service to Barnabas and Saul. We may be sure that there was baptizing to be done in most of the places where Barnabas and Saul preached.

3. The Dragoman?

"But the word may express the fact that John Mark was able to set the apostles more free for their work of evangelizing" (Knowling, "Acts," p. 285). He may have made "arrangements for board, lodging, and travelling" (Furneaux, "Acts," p. 197). Evangelists to-day sometimes have advance agents, advertising or publicity men, singers, personal workers, Bible class leaders, and what not, a regular company. It is to-day often "Smith and party," "Jones and party." There is no reason to refuse to admit some business organization in this new enterprise. Whether they started out with money or not, the time came when Paul made his own support and that of his friends by working at his trade. There were no boards to care for the new missionaries. There is no evidence that the church at Antioch contemplated financial responsibility for the campaign. They evidently did not mean to underwrite the expenses of the mission band for whom they so fervently prayed, for Paul later expressly says that in the beginning the Philippians alone had a share with him in the mission enterprise (Phil. 4:15). That crown belongs to Philippi, not to Antioch. But there were business details of various kinds that demanded attention and Mark was ready for them.

4. **The Assistant Preacher?**

"As an assistant—in what? 'Also,' as I think, recalls most naturally 'preached the word'; and the answer would be that he assisted them in the declaration of the word" (Hackett, "Acts," p. 151). Hackett recognizes that he stands almost alone in this view. And yet it would be hard to deny that John Mark would be allowed to preach the Gospel as occasion offered. There may have been overflow meetings or crowds in front of the synagogues or after-meetings or meetings in the homes as at his mother's home in Jerusalem where he could well exercise his gifts as a preacher of the Gospel. It may be fairly asked why John Mark's position has to be precisely defined; why, in fact, there may not be an element of truth in all these points of view which are not at all contradictory. He was ready for any service that was required to help on the work, a man of all work for the party. One of the most needed tasks was to instruct the catechumens. Mark was one who "had not the same gift of preaching to the unconverted, but who had an excellent memory, and a full knowledge of all those great events which were being told among them; and he (Paul) turned over the 'catechumens' to this 'attendant' or 'minister.' Mark would take the inquirers aside, and in some quiet place he would begin to tell the story of the Gospel in detail. He would meet them again and again for as long as they were in the place" (Moulton, "From Egyptian Rubbish Heaps," 1916, p. 93).

5. **If Less Honor, Less Responsibility.**

There was this to be said from Mark's

standpoint. He was in no sense the head, or even a head, of the party. Somebody has to do the humbler tasks in Christian work. An army of generals and captains would not be very formidable. It is the man in the trenches who does the chief work after all if he executes it well. The sequel, however, makes it clear that the responsibility for this enterprise rested rather lightly on Mark's shoulders. He may not have found it as congenial as he had hoped. The little foxes eat away the vines. There is a dull drag that comes in humdrum work that tries the spirit. Many a young preacher balks at the petty details of scholarly pursuits and refuses to pay the price for great attainments by the slavish drudgery of prolonged application to real research. The dust and grime of the mine drive away the charm of the gold and the diamond.

6. Willing to Start at This Level.

But it must not be forgotten that John Mark did set out on this great tour as the mere "attendant" of Barnabas and Saul. That is all to his credit and is worth noting. It is a long way from flagman on a train to president of the railroad and yet men have traversed that path. The bell-boy may some day be the bank president. The student will become the professor. The tyro will become the expert. The boy in the pew will become the peerless preacher. The people at Nazareth could not get over their astonishment that "the carpenter" (Mark 6:3), as they knew Jesus, could be the rabbi whose fame was now upon the lips of all, or even the Messiah of promise as some dared to affirm. He was great first as carpenter before He came to be great as teacher and Master of men's hearts and lives. All young preachers have to start somewhere. Broadus used to say that the only way to preach is to preach. One may learn all the theory of swimming and yet drown because he does not know how to swim. The door for the preacher to enter is the one that is open, not those that are closed.

IV

FLICKERING IN A CRISIS

"*Now Paul and his company set sail from Paphos, and came to Perga in Pamphylia: and John departed from them and returned to Jerusalem.*"

—ACTS 13: 13.

IV

FLICKERING IN A CRISIS

1. Deserting Paul and Barnabas at Perga.

MARK is kept distinctly in the background by Luke, for Paul is his hero in Acts 13 to 28. What did Mark think of the new situation that developed at Paphos and what was his subsequent conduct? We seldom act from single motives. One may be at the moment the strongest on the occasion for action, the last straw on the camel's back as we say, like the rebuke of Judas Iscariot by Christ at the feast in Bethany, but, once the spark is lighted, the other fagots add fuel to the flame. At Perga in Pamphylia John Mark (John, his Jewish name, Luke calls him here and in 13:5; but Mark, his Roman name, in 15:39, and both in 12:12, 25; 15:37), suddenly left the party and went back, not to Antioch, but to Jerusalem. Luke proffers no explanation of any kind, but shows later (15: 37–39) that Paul strongly resented what he considered Mark's desertion of the work in a crisis. Luke makes a colorless report of Mark's conduct at this stage: "John departed from them and returned to Jerusalem." There was a sharp cleavage[1] and a return[2] home. But in 15:38 Paul, as we shall see, practically accused Mark of apostasy[3] from the work which he had undertaken. Mark may not have foreseen the serious results that were to follow this act of his. There was probably some petulance and heat on his part, a "flare-up" when he left. He was clearly unwilling to go on and was not offering his resignation in order to be asked to withdraw it and stay with the party. It is always a serious question for a pastor to offer his resignation. He is not always able to see all sides of the problem. People are not always frank and sincere with him. Some will urge him to stay who really wish him to go. Some will say nothing who secretly

[1] *ἀποχωρήσας ἀπ' αὐτῶν.* These words accent the separation.

[2] *ὑπέστρεψεν* the same word employed in 12:25 of the return from Jerusalem to Antioch.

[3] *ἀποστάντα.*

hope that he will go. A noisy minority may override the will of the majority. But a pastor can stay too long as he can go too soon. It is easy to be too sensitive and then not to be sensitive enough. Many a young minister injures his whole ministerial career by not making good in his first pastorate and finds it hard to get another pastorate. Once out he has difficulty in getting in again. Mark takes an almost fatal step and quits all of a sudden and goes home as a returned missionary. He is in an embarrassing position at once. Many a young minister has found the work at college or at seminary surprisingly hard and has suddenly thrown up his scholastic training. He dodges Perga for a short-cut into the ministry. Mark never forgot Perga. It haunted him through the years. What made him quit at Perga? Paul and Barnabas were also at Perga and went on. Why did Mark turn back? They all faced the same difficulties, the same obstacles. There are two ways to treat obstacles in one's path, to turn back or to climb over them. Napoleon said, "There shall be no Alps," and went over the top into Italy. Mark turned back.

2. **Irritation at Paul's Preëminence.**

At Paphos "Saul, who is also called Paul" (Acts 13:9), took the lead and sternly rebuked Elymas Barjesus, the Jewish sorcerer, and broke his power over Sergius Paulus, the proconsul. The result was tremendous. Elymas was smitten with blindness and "he went about seeking some one to lead him by the hand" (13:11) and the proconsul "believed, being astonished at the teaching of the Lord" (13:12). But now also "Paul and his company set sail from Paphos" (13:13). It is significant that from now on Luke usually has "Paul" instead of "Saul" and that this forward step on Paul's part takes place in connection with a man named "Paulus." These two "Pauls" faced each other in the court at Paphos and the preacher won the proconsul, the first man in rank in Cyprus. "St. Paul generally accepted a scene before the authorities as bringing his work in a city to an end" (Rackham, "Acts," p. 203). At any rate Paul is now the leader,[1] though Barnabas had been specifically named as head of

[1] *οἱ περὶ Παῦλον*. This ancient Greek idiom neatly sets forth Paul ("those around Paul") as the center of the party. Cf. Robertson, "Grammar of the Greek New Testament in the Light of Historical Research," p. 620.

the expedition in the call of the Holy Spirit (13 : 2). "The young cousin felt a jealousy to which the generous Barnabas was himself superior" (Furneaux, "Acts," p. 203). Clearly Barnabas exhibited no chagrin at the new power that Paul displayed and rejoiced in his prowess. It is good when an older minister can rejoice at the achievements of the more gifted younger man whom he has helped to get a start. "In nothing is the greatness of Barnabas more manifest than in his recognition of the superiority of Paul and acceptance of a secondary position for himself" (Furneaux, *ibid.*). But Mark probably felt resentment on Barnabas' account and may have showed it. These little jealousies appeared among the twelve apostles during Christ's ministry and ministers to-day are subject to them like other men. The occasions for them test one's caliber. This spirit is sometimes a defect of a great man, though usually the sign of a weak one.

3. **The Change of Plan.**

Findlay (Hastings' Dictionary of the Bible, art. Paul) suggests that the repetition of the phrase " the work" (13 : 2; 14 : 26; 15 : 38) in Luke's narrative shows that the whole campaign had been mapped out before leaving Antioch. At any rate there was a change of leaders. Cyprus was the old home of Barnabas and the visit there was probably his suggestion. What is now Paul's plan? Rackham ("Acts," p. 205) thinks that Paul really wanted to go to Ephesus as he sought to go in the second journey (Acts 16 : 6) and hoped to find a ship at Perga for Ephesus. Ramsay ("St. Paul the Traveller and Roman Citizen," pp. 89 f.) holds that Pamphylia was to be the sphere of work among a people somewhat like those in Cilicia, Syria, and Cyprus where Paul had already labored. Ramsay suggests that Paul contracted the malaria at Perga from the mosquitoes on the Cestrus River and hence made a radical change of plan to go on and up through the dangerous mountain passes to Antioch in Pisidia where he could recover from the malaria on the elevated plateau (3,600 feet above sea level). He appeals to Galatians 4 : 13 f. as proof of this view which is on the basis of the South Galatian theory that Paul in Galatians is writing to the churches in Pisidia and Lycaonia established during this first tour. Ramsay holds that the sickness referred to by Paul in Galatians 4 : 13 f. as the occasion of his preaching in Galatia began in Perga. He also interprets "the splinter [1] in the flesh" (2 Cor. 12 : 7 f.) as the recurring attacks of malaria (the sudden chills or spasms) which humiliated him before the heathen who interpreted these spells as punishments from the gods. At any rate a change of plan seems to have been made at Perga. If Paul decided to go to Antioch in Pisidia for his health Mark may have interpreted it "as an abandonment of the work" (Knowling, "Acts," p. 289). This would be a possible retort to Paul's charge that Mark had deserted the work. Certainly a division of opinion arose and Mark refused to go further along the new path. He could say that he had not agreed to go to Pisidia and Lycaonia and be technically correct.

4. Paul's Aggressive Attitude Toward Gentiles.

We do not have to say that it was merely

[1] "And he told me that you had a sore foot owing to a splinter" *καὶ εἶπέ μοι ὅτι τὸν πόδαν πονεῖς ἀπὸ σκολάπου* (B. G. U. 380 iii. A. D.). This sentence occurs in the letter of an anxious mother who has heard of the injury to her son's foot.

a personal matter on Mark's part. He probably sympathized to some extent with the standpoint of the Pharisaic element in Jerusalem. Peter himself required a vision from the Lord to enable him to go to Cornelius in Cæsarea and to preach a free Gospel to him and his household. Even there Peter was openly apologetic (Acts 10:28) and only there perceived that God would save Gentiles without their becoming Jews (10:34) and in Jerusalem made it plain that God had opened the door to the Romans in Cæsarea (11:1–18). Barnabas had firmly maintained the freedom of the Greek Christians in Antioch from Jewish observances (11:23 ff.). But Paul's aggressive spirit seems to have longed for a great drive for the Gentiles whether the Jews responded or not. Precisely that situation arose in Antioch in Pisidia and Mark may have foreseen it or suspected it. "Seeing ye thrust it from you, and judge yourselves unworthy of eternal life, lo, we turn to the Gentiles" (Acts 14:46). "We conclude then that Mark was unable to keep pace with the rapid expansion of St. Paul's views of work in the Gentile world" (Rackham, "Acts," p. 204).

Mark may have intimated that the conversion of Sergius Paulus had made Paul willing to neglect the chosen people.

5. Hazards of the Hills Ahead.

Paul himself seems to refer to this period of his life when he speaks of "perils of rivers," "perils of robbers," and "perils in the wilderness" (2 Cor. 11 : 26). Various inscriptions in this region between Perga and Antioch in Pisidia tell of escape from drowning in a torrent swollen by rain, of a policeman slain by robbers, of armed policemen whose duty it was to capture runaway slaves (often the very worst brigands). "The roads all over the Roman Empire were apt to be unsafe, for the arrangements for insuring public safety were exceedingly defective; but probably the part of his life which St. Paul had most in mind when he wrote about the perils of rivers and of robbers, which he had faced in his journeys, was the journey from Perga across Taurus to Antioch and back again" (Ramsay, "The Church in the Roman Empire," 1893, p. 24). It is easy to see how Mark could argue that he had not agreed to go into such hazards. If it was springtime, he would hear of swollen streams and of bands of brigands. Besides, it was not his expedition anyhow. The Holy Spirit had not named him in the call which Barnabas and Saul had received. Mark "was a young man, and had perhaps entered on the work without counting the cost" (Furneaux, "Acts," p. 203). He had put his hand to the plow, but was now looking back. The furrow was running on too far for him. Mark was not a coward, but he was faint-hearted and his spirit quailed as he contemplated the real and imaginary dangers involved in a trip across the Taurus mountains through almost trackless forests. The brigands there were more dangerous than the wild beasts. Perhaps the heart of many a missionary has suffered like terrors as he came face to face with the grim realities of his life-work. Paul had much to say to Timothy about enduring hardness as a soldier of the cross. "Suffer hardship with me, as a good soldier of Christ Jesus" (2 Tim. 2:3). Paul was a true soldier and captain. He did not ask his followers to do what he was unwilling to share with them. But Paul had no patience with the tenderfoot. He wanted a real man to stand in his place in the trenches. "For God gave us not a spirit of fearfulness; but of power and love and discipline. Be not ashamed therefore of the testimony of our Lord, nor of me his prisoner: but suffer hardship with the Gospel according to the power of God" (2 Tim. 1:7 f.). This is Paul's message to all men who are tempted to be slackers or quitters in the ministry.

6. **Homesickness.**

Certainly he went home. He "returned to Jerusalem." Holtzmann says that he went home "to his mother" (zu seiner Mutter). A ship may have been about to sail from Perga to Cæsarea and Mark could not resist the impulse to depart (J. Robertson, "Scenes from the Life of St. Paul," p. 112). Swete ("Commentary," p. xiii) thinks "that duty to his mother and his home required him to break off at this point from so perilous a development of the mission." Depression probably combined with the other influences already mentioned and the action, once taken, was irrevocable. He was off for home and Paul and Barnabas were off for Antioch in Pisidia. It is even possible that Mark himself had a touch of malaria at Perga. If that was true, it was the decisive thing with him. He would go home and get out of all this entanglement. Malaria and homesickness make a powerful combination and go far toward unnerving a man for real work. When the physical energy is sapped, one's will has to fight the battle. Paul fought for the hills to go on with his work. Mark fled home to see his mother and let the work go. Mark undoubtedly loved his mother as he ought to have done, but it is an open question whether Mary was wholly glad to see him come back alone. To be sure, he had his story, but it was only one side of the matter. Mary had felt pride in seeing her son go out under the tutelage of two such preachers as Barnabas and Saul. There was, no doubt, a pang of disappointment in her heart as she saw him come home, especially when she learned of Paul's disapproval and that Barnabas had gone on with Paul. Life is full of complex problems that are hard to solve. The skein gets tangled and the temper becomes exasperated till we cut the Gordian knot and then we may cut it in the wrong place. There are thousands of young ministers who will understand John Mark's feelings as he journeyed home. Had he done right after all? What was he to do now? A young minister quits his college or seminary course under provocation or in despair at the difficulties met at Perga. He resigns his first pastorate because of a sudden clash with some member of the church or because the work seems unusually hard or the remuneration inadequate or the people indifferent or the climate unsuitable. A young missionary suddenly flings up his work and comes home and finds himself in a very embarrassing position. He is not a hero to others and his courage is gone. A Y. M. C. A. secretary in the army camps has to take his lot with the men in camp and at the front. If he is overly particular, he will not have the respect of the men whom he is trying to help. We all meet Perga, but Paul went on to victory and power.

V

THROWN OUT OF WORK

"*And Barnabas was minded to take with them John also, who was called Mark.*"—ACTS 15 : 37.

V

THROWN OUT OF WORK

1. A Spectator, Not a Fighter.

MARK is dropped by Luke till we come to Antioch again in Acts 15: 36–41. Much water has run under the mill in the meanwhile. Paul and Barnabas finished their great tour as far as Derbe and then returned to Antioch in Syria where "they rehearsed all things that God had done with them, and that he had opened a door of faith unto the Gentiles" (Acts 14:27). It was a veritable missionary triumph and echoes of this great event reached Jerusalem and led certain self-appointed leaders, "to whom we gave no commandment" (Acts 15:24), to go up to Antioch to file formal protest against this great Gentile propaganda by Paul and Barnabas. One of the great issues in the history of Christianity was sprung and Paul did not hesitate a moment to champion the cause of spiritual freedom for the Gentile Christians against the bondage of Pharisaism which the Judaizing Christians from Jerusalem wished to impose upon them. Luke reports the conflict in Acts 15: 1–35 and Paul has a sketch of the private aspects of the controversy in Galatians 2: 1–10. Mark was undoubtedly a spectator of what was going on in Jerusalem and had his own point of view about it all. But, alas, instead of being in the thick of it with Paul and Barnabas, as he might have been, he is now an outsider. There must have been some bitterness of spirit as Mark saw the fresh honors coming to the leaders whom he had deserted at Perga. No honor came to Mark.

2. Sympathy with the Judaizers.

It is almost certain that Mark had a reaction of feeling from Paul to Peter, as he understood Peter, when the controversy started. Everybody was taking sides. The Pharisaic party in the Jerusalem church (Acts 11: 2; 15: 1 f.) felt certain that Peter and James would take their side against Paul. It is hardly proper to say that Mark aligned himself openly with the Judaizers for

Paul calls them "false brethren" (Gal. 2:4) and Barnabas stood with Paul and that fact would have a restraining influence on Mark. But many a minister, who has been temporarily thrown out of work, has had the temptation to bitterness of spirit and sourness of disposition that finds expression in unpleasant remarks about other ministers. The man who is "down and out" easily becomes a "knocker" against the man who is still at work. The keenest critic is the one who is doing nothing else. The man who becomes an incarnate sneer toward his brethren will find it hard to be just. It would be easy for Mark to find ample justification for his own withdrawal from the Gentile propaganda of Paul in the ugly things that the Judaizers were saying, things that Mark would not say himself, but which he probably took no pains to contradict. He could at least point to the strife that had been caused and that could have been avoided by a more moderate and cautious campaign. Perhaps he could say, "I told you so."

3. Silenced by Victory.

But victory has a quieting effect upon

many people. The noise of the Judaizers was great at the start (Acts 15 : 5), but Peter and even James had championed the cause of Gentile freedom as expounded by Paul and Barnabas (15 : 7–21) and in the end the vote in favor of the resolution by James, the president of the conference, was unanimous (15 : 22), the Judaizers themselves probably not voting when they saw that they were in a hopeless minority. For the second time, therefore, the Judaizers were silenced; once in the arraignment of Simon Peter (11 : 18) to which event Peter skillfully referred in his speech for Paul (15 : 7), and now in the triumph of Paul and Barnabas. They are sullen and sulk in their tents and wait for another occasion to renew the strife. Men of this type will not keep the spirit of an agreement. Documents and "decrees" (Acts 16:4) are mere "scraps of paper" in their eyes when they are bent on carrying their point in the end. But, no doubt, Mark was duly impressed by the victory of Paul and Barnabas. Mark was bound to review the whole situation in the light of the new developments. Since the policy of the whole of Christendom was now settled on the question of the freedom of the Gentiles from Jewish ceremonialism, Mark's opposition was probably gone. The question was at least settled and he was ready to join in the work again. "The remonstrance of Barnabas may have brought him to a sense of his previous misconduct" (Furneaux, "Acts," p. 250). Thus Mark's prejudices may have vanished.

4. In Antioch Again.

At any rate we see Mark in Antioch again and with Barnabas. It is not quite clear on what basis he came. He may have come up with Simon Peter whose visit to Antioch led to the unfortunate episode which Paul relates in Galatians 2:11–21. This visit of Peter was apparently after the Jerusalem conference, though Ramsay makes it before, and the same as the visit of the Judaizers in Acts 15:1 ("St. Paul the Traveller," p. 158). If we take Galatians 2:1–10 to refer to the same meeting as Acts 15:4–29, we have to put Peter's visit later. So we can imagine Peter in Antioch with Paul and Barnabas after the great victory in Jerusalem. Peter "ate with the Gentiles" (Gal. 2:12) as he was accused by the Pharisaic Christians of doing at

Cæsarea (Acts 11 : 3). The question of social relations did not come up in the Jerusalem conference and the "certain" ones from Jerusalem "from James" claimed that Peter had gone beyond that agreement and that James would not approve this step of Peter. It is even possible that Mark was one of these "certain" ones, but not likely. Peter, however, was so much impressed by them, "fearing them of the circumcision," that he recanted and changed his conduct to the disgust and the indignation of Paul who "resisted him to the face" "before *them* all." Certainly Paul did not regard Peter as the Pope. The worst of it was that "the rest of the Jews dissembled likewise with him, insomuch that even Barnabas was carried away by their dissimulation" (Gal. 2 : 13). Paul used a hard word "hypocrisy"[1] to describe this conduct of Peter and "even Barnabas." *Et tu, Brute.* How did Barnabas come to waver and to desert Paul after all their struggles together and after their recent victory in Jerusalem and after the joyful ratification in Antioch (Acts 15 : 31)? The most plausible explanation is John Mark's influence on Barnabas, who may

[1] τῇ ὑποκρίσει.

have persuaded him that James really was opposed to the social equality between Greek and Jewish Christians which was practiced at Antioch and which Paul and Barnabas had also practiced on their recent tour. The defection of Peter and all the other Jewish Christians in Antioch left Barnabas and Paul alone on this point. Example is powerful upon most of us. So Barnabas stepped over to the side of Peter and left Paul alone, *Paulus contra mundum*. At last Barnabas had renounced Paul's leadership to the joy of John Mark.

5. Won Back to Paul.

Paul is silent about Mark. Luke does not say how it was done. But it is evident that Paul won Peter and Barnabas quickly to his view again. The breach was momentary and was soon healed. It was all a mistake about James and Mark is brought once again to feel kindly toward Paul. It is not likely that Paul was told if there was any change in the feeling of Mark in the matter, but we know that Mark was willing to coöperate with Paul again for he allows Barnabas to mention the matter to Paul. This speaks well for Mark and shows that he had not become wholly embittered by what had occurred. Mark had probably never said that he would not work again with Paul. If he had said it, he took it back. A man can always do that if he is a real man. It is a little man who can never unsay what he has said that is wrong, who is the slave of consistency and of his own mistakes. It is never too late to mend and to own that one was wrong.

6. Renominated by Barnabas.

It is almost certain that Mark was taken along in the first tour on the initiative of Barnabas. The wound was soon healed, as has been said, between Paul and Barnabas who was a generous soul and who really loved Paul. The spirit of Paul ere long yearned to go back to the work. He longed to see again the faces of the brethren and sisters who had been won to Christ in the first tour (Acts 15 : 36). So Paul made a formal offer to Barnabas that they two go out again on a second tour among the Gentiles. It was only fitting that these two men should go together again. Barnabas was more than willing, only "he was minded to take with them John also, who was called Mark." Once again, then, Barnabas proposed Mark. Paul had not asked for Mark. It is always a delicate matter, this thing of proposing the right man for a certain task. Somebody has to do the work. Somebody has to nominate men for work in church, state, school, business. But it is not an easy thing to do wisely. Plenty of men "are mentioned," but few can really measure up to the highest places. The attitude of pulpit committees before a call is extended to a pastor and afterwards is very remarkable. So, now and then, a preacher is found who is eager to step into the highest place whether desired or not. But it is not hard to read between the lines here and to see that Mark had not been happy since he left Perga. There are few sadder things than the minister who feels called to preach and yet nobody seems called to listen to him. He seems a ministerial misfit and is not expected to go into business. But he must make an honest living. Paul had no such clerical scruples as we have to-day. He resolutely made his own living by his trade with his own hands and refused to starve because a church like that at Corinth would not pay for his work. Paul had the world before him and, when persecuted in one city, he went on to the next. To-day we have, in self-defense, to know a man's antecedents if he comes as a stranger before we dare open our churches to him. This is one of the drawbacks of work in a highly organized Christianity. But Barnabas boldly championed the cause of John Mark and made it his own. He wanted to give him another trial. Probably Mark "was prepared to promise greater perseverance" (Furneaux, "Acts," p. 250). It was necessary that Mark be reinstated somehow and get on his feet again. He had made a great mistake. But was he to be damned forever for that? Who does not sometimes make a mistake? We can imagine how the mind of Barnabas worked in a truly sympathetic vein as he plead the cause of Mark. Our hearts are with Barnabas in this plea as they go out to every young minister who stumbles and tries to get up again and to go on in the work to which he feels called. There was Peter himself, a man of impulse and of power. Jesus forgave Peter and sent a special message of reinstatement to him and made him chief spokesman at Pentecost. Peter had fallen and Christ had raised him up. Mark deserved to be given a new opportunity and Barnabas was the man to help him. Had not Barnabas befriended Paul when he was distrusted by all the saints in Jerusalem? Paul was under great obligations to Barnabas who had also brought him to Antioch and had thus given him his great opportunity for service. How could Paul resist such a plea from Barnabas?

VI

TURNED DOWN BY PAUL

"*But Paul thought not good to take with them him who withdrew from them from Pamphylia, and went not with them to the work.*"—Acts 15 : 38.

VI

TURNED DOWN BY PAUL

1. Paul's Surprise at Barnabas.

IT was Barnabas who had proposed Mark for the first tour which led to the sad defection at Perga. And now Barnabas was suggesting his cousin again. It looked to Paul like nepotism. Partiality to relatives in posts of responsibility is not relished by the public in church or state affairs (Stalker, "The Life of St. Paul," p. 119). And Barnabas insisted[1] on taking John Mark "also," as Luke vividly describes it. Paul had become accustomed to the leadership by now and this sudden independence on the part of Barnabas came as a jolt. "It may even be that Barnabas, after finding himself once more in the old place of high consideration at Jerusalem was beginning to feel his secondary position at Antioch, and resented

[1] ἐβούλετο imperfect tense (continued action).

Paul's determination to have his own way" (Furneaux, "Acts," pp. 250f.). Barnabas probably felt also that it was unjust to ruin the career of a young man like Mark because of a mistake of which he was now sincerely sorry. But Paul could retort that this goodness of Barnabas to John Mark was in fact nothing but good-natured weakness (Johnston, "St. Paul and His Mission to the Roman Empire," p. 99). Paul probably felt also that Barnabas was presuming on their old and tried friendship in pressing Mark upon him and so stood his ground.[1] He felt (Hackett, "Acts," p. 179) that Barnabas was influenced more by his feelings than by his judgment. And yet Paul esteemed Barnabas very highly. It was just this love for Barnabas that hurt him so when the cleavage came. At the time of the temporary defection of Peter and Barnabas Paul said, "even Barnabas," strong proof of his high esteem (Lightfoot, on Galatians 2 : 13).

2. Indignation at Mark.

As we have seen, the recent conduct of Mark had stirred again Paul's resentment

[1] ἠξίου. Imperfect against imperfect (ἐβούλετο).

toward him for his desertion at Perga. He had certainly stood with Peter and Barnabas and the rest of the Jews against Paul at Antioch. He had probably sympathized at first with the Judaizers and Paul was distinctly prejudiced against him. "Paul deemed it worth while or proper not to be taking along this fellow, the one who apostatized from them from Pamphylia and did not go with them to the work." This is a literal translation of Luke's language about Paul.[1] Paul thought of the misery of having this deserter (apostate[2]) from his friends, though not from Christ, hanging around all the time and liable to prove fickle again and to quit, this fellow who would not stick to the work and left his co-workers in the lurch in the pinch at Perga. John took his hand from the plow and was not worthy to be entrusted with that plow again. Evidently Paul was not sure of Mark's real sympathy with the Gentile propaganda. He might fly off the handle again and greatly embarrass Paul

[1] Barnabas is pictured as proposing *συνπαραλαβεῖν* (aorist, punctiliar) while Paul speaks of it as *συνπαραλαμβάνειν* (present, linear).

[2] *τὸν ἀποστάντα.*

with the churches in South Galatia. "He could not trust a staff which had once broken in his hand" (Furneaux, "Acts," p. 252). Mark had been disloyal to the mission among the Gentiles. Paul could base his opposition, therefore, on the interests of the cause rather than on his own personal likes and dislikes. If Mark went along and was once more unfaithful, Paul would hold Barnabas doubly responsible.

3. **Sharp Contention Between Paul and Barnabas.**

The word employed by Luke is our very word "paroxysm."[1] Probably neither meant the thing to go that far, but suppressed emotion and hitherto unexpressed convictions now came to the surface. The gentle Barnabas, son of consolation, was now violent in a dispute. Paul may have chided him with being too tolerant of faint-heartedness (Pressensé, "The Early Years of Christianity," p. 113). He could now retort that Paul was too hard-hearted and unsympathetic. "The smaller rubs of life often try the temper more than

[1] *παροξυσμός*. *Ὀξύς* means "sharp" like vinegar and *ὀξύνω* to make sharp and *παρά* intensifies the idea.

the greater things, and they find us with our armor off" (Furneaux, "Acts" p. 250). Paul may have wondered how Barnabas really felt about his leadership. The wound seemed healed after his rebuke of Peter and Barnabas, but it is easy to open an old sore. Perhaps after all Barnabas was not willing to go whole-heartedly and to the logical conclusion with Paul in the mission work among the Gentiles. Luke does not hesitate to reveal the sad fact of the bitterness between these two old friends about John Mark, but he does not preserve the sharp words used by either Paul or Barnabas. It is just as well not to know them. Probably both men deeply regretted some things that they said, however true they were. It is not necessary to decide who was right in the controversy. There was undoubtedly right on both sides. There is no way to settle our likes and dislikes about persons. The only way out is to agree to disagree. It is partly temperament and it is well that people do differ so.

4. Separation Between Paul and Barnabas. It is sad to see these great apostles of the Gentiles part. Furneaux ("Acts," p. 252) thinks that they may have known each other as fellow students at Tarsus. Certainly their lives had been strangely linked together and each had done much for the other. Barnabas had been Paul's best friend among the Christians and had championed his sincerity from the start (Acts 9 : 27) and had faced with him the perils of rivers and of robbers from which John Mark shrank. He had shared Paul's perils with the heathen and had fought by his side against the false brethren who had tried to undo his world-work. And now they must part. These two men were the outstanding figures in the mission work of the early Christians. The worst of it was that they parted in anger. If Paul was parting from his chief benefactor, Barnabas was leaving the foremost spirit of his time (Stalker, "The Life of St. Paul," p. 120). "They parted asunder from one another."[1] They never worked together again and, so far as we know, never met again. The breach was later healed, we may be sure, for Paul speaks kindly of Barnabas in 1 Corinthians 9 : 6, and Colossians 4 : 10. We may be sure that Paul felt a keen pang over this parting from Barnabas. Had

[1] ὥστε ἀποχωρισθῆναι αὐτοὺς ἀπ' ἀλλήλων.

he done right after all? Who can tell? He will later say: "Love is not provoked,"[1] and will use this very word for "paroxysm." Will he be thinking of his sad experience by which he had learned this truth? In Acts 17:16 Luke uses this same word for the provocation of Paul's spirit at the sight of so many idols in Athens. We are exhorted in Hebrews 10:24 to "consider one another for a paroxysm of love and of good works," this word again. Provocation may be to good or to evil and God can overrule the evil and turn it into good. At any rate "two missionary bands started instead of one, and new workers were taken into the field" (Rackham, "Acts," p. 261). Barnabas went his way and Paul went his. Luke follows the fortunes of Paul and Barnabas drops out of sight in Acts. The so-called Epistle of Barnabas is not genuine. Some consider him the author of the Epistle to the Hebrews. Of that we do not know. "We part from the honorable and gracious personality of Barnabas with deep regret; but history marches with Paul" (Ramsay, "Pictures of the Apostolic Church," p. 198).

[1] 1 Corinthians 13:5 οὐ παροξύνεται.

5. Paul and Silas.

Silas did not take the place of Mark, but of Barnabas. Paul felt no need of Mark and had no place for him and chose no successor to him. Silas had been sent with Judas from Jerusalem to bear the Epistle from the Conference to the church in Antioch (Acts 15:32). Silas is an abbreviation for Silvanus (1 Thess. 1:1; 2 Thess. 1:1; 2 Cor. 1:19). Like Paul, he was a Roman citizen (Acts 16:37). He was loyal to Paul through the second tour and yet was on intimate terms with Peter (1 Pet. 5:12). He was a Hellenistic Jew like Paul and a worthy successor to Barnabas. He had apparently remained in Antioch after coming up and was in full sympathy with Paul's views of work among the Gentiles. The sympathy of the church at Antioch was apparently with Paul and Silas as they start upon the new campaign, "being commended by the brethren to the grace of the Lord" (Acts 15:40).

6. Mark's Meditations.

Barnabas apparently had already gone away with Mark to Cyprus. Did Mark have no compunctions of conscience over being the occasion of this cleavage between Paul and Barnabas? We can only conjecture his thoughts as he sailed away with Barnabas. Should a preacher allow a church to be divided over him? That question cannot be easily answered. It all depends. Jesus Himself has brought division into many homes. He brings peace beyond all understanding, but sometimes the sword comes first. But no sincere preacher enjoys being a bone of contention between opposing factions, least of all being the cause of bitterness between the closest friends. Many a preacher has known what it is to be rejected by church committees and by churches themselves. It is not a pleasant experience to be a candidate for a vacant pulpit and to be passed by. Marcus Dods was a probationer for six years after he graduated at New College before he received a call to be pastor. Church after church invited him to preach and then rejected him. Such an experience would have embittered the spirit of a narrow man, but Dods utilized these years to make a scholar of himself. In time he became the principal of New College and a glory to Scotland. Surely it was now a crisis for John Mark. It is not pleasant to be a ministerial misfit. But one may be a misfit in one place and make a fit in another. Was there a place that Mark would suit? He had apparently lost his chance with Paul. He had lost the greatest opportunity. Would he make good in another sphere? The answer lies with Mark himself. The preacher who is always looking to his friends to save him from his own mistakes will reach the end of his tether.

VII

GIVEN A NEW CHANCE BY BARNABAS

"*And Barnabas took Mark with him, and sailed away unto Cyprus.*"—Acts 15: 39.

VII

GIVEN A NEW CHANCE BY BARNABAS

1. The Victim of Circumstances.

SURELY Mark was caught in the toils of circumstance not wholly in his control. At college we used to debate whether the man made the crisis or the crisis the man. Certainly there is an element of truth in both. Man is not a mere machine driven by blind fate. He has will and choice and within limits is the arbiter of his own career and makes his own destiny. An unstable man can find plenty of excuses for his own fickleness and failures, usually in the capricious whims of other people and the general perversity of things. Such men talk of luck and blind fate and not of pluck and good Providence. It is too much to expect that, as yet, John Mark held himself responsible for what had happened to him. Other men have had like difficulty in seeing their own situation. Pessimism comes at times to the noblest spirits. Marcus Dods was mentioned in the preceding chapter as a noble specimen of the young minister who held himself to the highest things and went on with his studies, though the churches would not have him. Some found this fault with him and some that, sometimes directly contradictory faults. It was so with John the Baptist and with Jesus. Marcus Dods stuck to his Greek and Hebrew and went on learning and growing till his day should come. It was long in coming and there were dark hours. Toward the close of his six years of probation he wrote to his sister who was his confidant and comfort: "I am feeling more and more done, and if this Glasgow thing comes to nothing, I don't see why or how I am to hang on longer; physically I cannot and morally and spiritually I have been done long ago. I never preached better than at Glasgow; it is a nice church, very, but only about 180 people, so that each might have had a pew. This, of course, makes the idea of a call rather terrific, as how could I ever increase them?" ("Early Letters of Marcus Dods," p. 186).

Then later he writes (*ibid.*, p. 199) that "Dr. Bonar has been at me again, not for Naples, but for Sydney. He tells me what he told me before that Dr. Mackay there wants a colleague, and that no placed minister here who is fit will go." Dods began to examine himself to see what was the matter. "If I could get a man to put warmth into me, and utterance, in Paul's sense, I would deliver wonderfully. But it vexes me all the more when people talk of my delivery, for I feel all the more deeply it is not an external thing that art can overcome, but my nature that is not a preacher's nature" (*ibid.*, p. 195). "There is no chance henceforth for the like of me, you know, and what I say to myself I say also to you" (*ibid.*, p. 293). "I am not so envious, I think, as you have known me; it comes back upon me, but rather as an old memory than as a present habit" (*ibid.*, p. 294). And yet Marcus Dods became one of the great preachers of his day and a teacher of preachers who has left his stamp upon a whole generation of young ministers. Perga had once overcome John Mark. Would he now triumph over Perga?

2. The Duty of a Kinsman.

It is certain that Barnabas felt a sort of responsibility for the success of John Mark's ministry that Paul did not share. He was his kinsman and that fact did impose an extra burden upon his shoulders. Paul will later refer to Mark as "the cousin of Barnabas"[1] (Col. 4:10) in a way that "reads like a fond recollection of old times" (Furneaux, "Acts," p. 252) and that seems partly explanatory also of the fact that Mark's life had been more closely identified with that of Barnabas than with that of Paul. Blood relationship does not justify favoritism, but neither does it absolve one from his peculiar obligations. We may well believe that Barnabas cherished no grudge against Paul for what he considered his harsh, even unkind, treatment of Mark. He was too high-minded and warm-hearted a man to nourish resentment. The world was wide and there was work enough for all and personal prejudices must not be allowed to sour one's temper. But, all the same, Paul's scornful rejection of Mark as a co-worker naturally intensified the devotion of Barnabas to his protégé and dis-

[1] ὁ ἀνεψιὸς Βαρνάβα.

ciple. He at least must do his part by Mark and see to it that he has another chance in which to redeem himself and show that he could make good after all, that he had the stuff of manhood in him. It must be admitted that kinspeople do not always stand by one when he is down and out. Too often they are the severest critics of all and do least to set one on his feet again. A sense of mortification ofttimes makes one's kinspeople really unkind and unduly hard. It must be confessed that one can strain to the snapping point the chords of love and yet blood is blood and love is love. Blessings be upon Barnabas, the man of heart, who was unwilling to throw to the scrap-heap this fine young minister without one more trial. Barnabas could at least feel that he had done his duty by John Mark. The minister who has failed is taboo with many churches and preachers. The excuses may be excellent, but nothing succeeds like success and nothing fails like failure. In war the general who loses a campaign loses also his official head. We are all willing for people to learn how to rectify their mistakes, provided they do their learning upon somebody else. An old preacher requires something of a mother's love and tender patience to deal with the crudities of youth and the clinging tendrils of young hearts that reach out after the sturdy oak by which to climb. One must not victimize other churches just to help a kinsman get a start. A delicate sense of loyalty to the cause of Christ is involved as well as the desire to be of service to a young minister who has missed the path of usefulness.

3. Sympathy with the Weaker Brother.

Mark's conduct at Perga probably did not appear to Barnabas in the light of a desertion. We go in the end of the day by the bent of our natures. Joseph was nicknamed (surnamed) Barnabas by the apostles because of his great generosity. He sold a field in the hour of need in Jerusalem and laid the money at the feet of the apostles (Acts 4:36f.). That soubriquet, son of consolation, supplanted the name of Joseph just as Cephas or Peter did that of Simon. He lived up to his surname and never appears to better advantage than when he is befriending a brother in trouble. "We must never forget that twice over did Barnabas save Saul for the work of Christianity" (Knowling, "Acts," p. 331). As he had befriended Saul when he had no friends in Jerusalem, so he now takes John Mark under his protecting care. "Barnabas took[1] Mark with him and sailed away unto Cyprus." This was an act of courage and of kindness of heart that was wholly in keeping with the generous nature of Barnabas. Paul and Barnabas said to the men of Lystra who tried to worship them as Mercury and Jupiter: "We are men of like nature with you" (Acts 14:15). The milk of human kindness was abundant in the heart of Barnabas. After all is said, there is nothing that will take the place of sympathy in a preacher. This is true, of course, in his preaching. Broadus used to say that, as Demosthenes stressed "action, action, action" as the three most important things in the speaker, so he would emphasize "sympathy, sympathy, sympathy" as the three prime requisites in the preacher of the Gospel. This is true of the pastoral side also. The shepherd heart is vital to the pastor. People must know that the pastor takes his

[1] παραλαβόντα took along.

place by their side as well as at their head. The captain who will go over the top with his men can lead them anywhere. Jesus is the only perfect man. In the Gospels the weaknesses of the disciples stand out in bold outline. We are all sinners. "We are all poor critters," Dr. Arthur Peter of Louisville, one of God's noblemen, used to say. There was no posing as perfect on the part of either Paul or Barnabas (Macduff, "The Footsteps of St. Paul," p. 157). Paul was only "a minister, a servant, a slave of Christ." Paul knew how to help other ministers. No other minister save Jesus our Lord has ever stimulated and stirred to the highest things ministers of the Gospel as has Paul of Tarsus. He was also a man of great heart and deep emotion. But in the case of John Mark it is Barnabas who shows the touch of nature that makes the whole world kin.

4. Barnabas Able Now to Tell Mark His Fault.

That is always a most delicate thing to do. If done unwisely, the work of correction may do more harm than good. The wound may be made deeper and may heal more slowly. And yet a skillful surgeon will cleanse the wound of all impurities so that it will heal. The probing may hurt for the moment. We may trust Barnabas for this part of the discipline of Mark. We may be sure that Barnabas would not make a hero or a martyr of Mark and allow him to nurse his grievance against Paul to the neglect of a vision of his own shortcoming. The parent has to walk this narrow path every day with the children and makes mistakes enough, now one way, now the other. The teacher finds it hard to strike the balance correctly, to praise properly and to correct discreetly. The school of experience is the one where all of us have to learn lessons that we will not or cannot learn elsewhere.

5. Learning by Mistakes.

Suffering plays a large part in all of the soul's progress. It pleased God, "in bringing many sons unto glory, to make the author of their salvation perfect through suffering" (Heb. 2:10). This great passage dignifies humanity and ennobles suffering as a means of teaching our souls the ways of God. Jesus had to live His human life before He could have the wealth of sympathy that gave Him power to succor the tempted (Heb. 2:18). The preacher has to tread the same road. Disappointment lies in his path. It is never too late to mend, if one will learn his lesson and learn to make the mistakes of his life stepping-stones to higher things. But one must first see one's error and acknowledge it as an error and resolve to change one's conduct. Fickleness will ruin the career of any man. A rolling stone gathers no moss, we say. It is clear from the sequel that Mark learned his lesson from Barnabas who proved a wise and loving teacher.

6. The Last Glimpse of Barnabas.

Back in Cyprus Barnabas was in his old home and Mark in that of his family. Ramsay ("Pictures of the Apostolic Church," p. 198) says that Barnabas "went away into the backwater of Cyprus and passes out of history." That is a rather curt way to dismiss Barnabas and Mark. Luke traced the fortunes of Paul who was undoubtedly a greater man than Barnabas or Mark. Barnabas had no biographer and wrote no letters that have been preserved. Clearly Luke did not estimate the work of Barnabas in the same category as that of Paul in the development of Christianity (Knowling, "Acts," p. 331). But Barnabas was not a negligible factor up to this period, Luke himself being witness. Indeed, he is distinctly one of the great figures in the early days of Christianity, up to the close of Acts 15. There is no reason to think that Barnabas was idle or in a sulk because of his separation from Paul. The tradition is that he died in Cyprus. He was an older man than Paul. The bulk of his work was probably already behind him, while Paul was now in his prime. Barnabas had done enough to make his name immortal. In Cyprus he was with old friends and he could confirm and consolidate the work already done there. He did not die right away because he is apparently still at work when Paul writes 1 Corinthians (9:6). He and Paul are still friends. If Barnabas had done nothing further during these years but save Mark, he would have accomplished a great work. The old preacher finds his chief joy in the fresh glow of enthusiasm of the young servant of Christ. Thus men die and the work goes on. Mark would not be an apprentice always. His days of probation were over. If he was ever to accomplish anything worth while, he must be at it. Some men develop more slowly than others. The infant prodigies are not always giants as adults. Some of those who ripen slowly are like oaks when grown to maturity. Mark had his gifts, though not of the very highest order, yet real and worth using to the full. Will he come to himself, get a grip on his powers, and get down to "brass-tacks," as we say? If so, he must be up and doing. He cannot spend all his days under the shadow of Barnabas' wing. The only way to preach is to preach. The only way to work is to work. Nothing will take the place of steady application. John D. Rockefeller gives "stick-to-ativeness" as one of the great rules of success in life. That rule applies to the ministry as to all other occupations. The touch-and-go preacher will leave little result when he goes. If one has to apologize always for the preacher's mistakes, he will by and by grow weary. The positive side of the scales must make a showing else one will be weighed in the balances and found wanting.

VIII

PETER'S SON AND INTERPRETER

"*Mark my son.*"—1 PETER 5 : 13.

"*Mark, having become the interpreter of Peter.*"
—Papias, quoted in Eusebius, H. E. III. 39.

VIII

PETER'S SON AND INTERPRETER

1. One of Peter's Converts.

THIS is a natural meaning of Peter's language "my son," though not necessarily so. Spiritual relationship of this kind is usually expressed by another word[1] in Paul's Epistles (Swete, "Commentary," p. xvi). Still, it is quite possible that Peter employed this word in the sense of spiritual sonship. We know that Peter was a welcome visitor to the house of Mary and he was probably the instrument of their conversion to Christ. It is curious to find McGiffert[2] ascribing 1 Peter to Barnabas because of this affectionate designation of John Mark. Surely Peter loved his converts as tenderly as did Paul. Nothing is more natural

[1] τέκνον (1 Cor. 4:7; Phil. 2:22; 1 Tim. 1:2; Titus 1:4, etc.), whereas Peter uses υἱός.

[2] "History of Christianity in the Apostolic Age," pp. 599 f.

than that Mark should be with Peter again if Peter was his spiritual father. It is not necessary to suppose that Mark remained with Barnabas till his death if Peter needed him and Barnabas had no further need of his services. He probably had already been one of Peter's pupils and Peter was only too glad to have his former disciple with him again, "who as a young disciple must often have sat at his feet to be catechized and taught the way of the Lord, and who had come to look upon his mother's old friend and teacher as a second father, and to render to him the offices of filial piety" (Swete, "Commentary," p. xvi).

2. A Congenial Atmosphere at Last.

Peter was sure to understand John Mark and he knew his family history, his gifts and temperament. The work with Peter was with the Jewish Christians, for he was the leader of this work as Paul of the Gentile mission (Gal. 2 : 9). Here Mark would have fewer scruples and could find ample play for his powers. All that was in him ought to come out. Mark was fortunate in his teachers. It is not every young preacher who falls under the tutelage of three men like Paul, Barnabas, and Peter. The best thing in any school is the personality of the teachers. One really great teacher in a school justifies the school. Pupils forget the lessons and make sport of their teachers, but some men they cannot forget. It is precisely so in the school of life. It is true that Mark found Paul a sterner and stricter teacher than Barnabas and Peter, but we must not imagine that Paul did not help Mark. Indeed, his very severity may have been the saving of Mark in the end. Chastisement does not seem good at the time, not even chastisement from the Lord (Heb. 12 : 11). There will come a time when we may be able to rejoice even in the chastisement. But life is not meant to be all chastisement. There is a joy of work that calls out the best that is in one. Some men are always disgruntled and are never satisfied with the task which they have. They imagine that they would be happy and useful somewhere else and at some other work. A restless spirit like that creates worry and unfits one for work of a high order. The cure may be in a change of sphere. More likely the cure can be found in doing heartily whatever one has to do. Joy in work comes, to be sure, from doing a thing well, but one may do well whatever is in hand and find joy in doing it better. The affectionate description of Mark by Peter proves that there was genuine camaraderie between these two men, master and disciple as they were. Confidence begets love. Fidelity begets confidence. It is clear, therefore, that now Mark was throwing his whole soul into the work with Simon Peter.

3. **The Time of the Work with Peter.**

There is doubt as to the precise time when he became firmly associated with Peter. Swete thinks that it was not till after Paul's death. That is hardly likely, for the Gospel of Mark was probably written in the fifties, certainly before the Gospel of Luke, which in turn was before the Acts, and Acts was written by A. D. 63 if Luke closes the book because events had only proceeded thus far. We may think therefore of Mark with Peter during most of the fifties and the early sixties. This was while Paul was doing his great work during the second and third mission tours, the imprisonment at Cæsarea and in Rome. He will meet Paul, as we shall see, toward the close of this period. There is no inconsistency in thinking of Mark as being of service to Paul while he was still the follower of Peter. The length of the stay with Peter is not known, for we do not know how long Mark was with Barnabas in Cyprus, but it may very well have been some dozen years or more. It was during this period that Mark wrote his Gospel, as we shall see, and so made his real contribution to Christianity. That grew directly out of his love for Peter and the heartiness of his coöperation with him.

4. Peter's Dragoman in His Journeys.

Papias expressly says that Mark followed not the Lord Jesus, but Peter.[1] Clement of Alexandria speaks of Mark as "one who had followed him for a long time."[2] Eusebius says that Mark "had become his familiar acquaintance and attendant."[3] Peter himself says that Mark is with him in Babylon when he writes the first Epistle (1 Pet. 5:13). The usual

[1] οὔτε γὰρ ἤκουσε τοῦ Κυρίου οὔτε παρηκολούθησεν αὐτῷ, ὕστερον δέ, ὡς ἔφην, Πέτρῳ.

[2] Hypot. in Eus. H. E. VI. 14.

[3] γνώριμος καὶ φοιτητής. Dem. Evang. III. 5.

opinion is that Rome is here meant by "Babylon," mystical Babylon, the great enemy of Christianity as in the Apocalypse. Already the disciples are persecuted as Christians (1 Pet. 4 : 16) and this was true from A. D. 46, the date of the burning of Rome by Nero who laid his own crime at the door of the Christians. There are many other proofs that Peter was in Rome and none that he was in Babylon, though that is the natural way to take his language.[1] However that may be, Peter was then near the close of his work and travels. He is writing to "the elect who are sojourners of the Dispersion in Pontus, Galatia, Cappadocia, Asia and Bithynia" (1 Pet. 1 : 1), regions where he had probably preached himself, thus covering a part of Paul's old territory. It is quite probable that Peter had Mark with him during these journeys. There are traditions also that Mark preached in Egypt. He is credited with some share in the founding of the church in Alexandria. But the testimony is very strong that in various parts of the world Mark was

[1] Swete considers it "highly improbable" that there were Jews enough in Babylon at this time to justify a visit from Peter ("Comm.," p. xvi).

Peter's "interpreter" or dragoman quite apart from the writing of the Gospel. Papias states it, as already noted, but so also does Tertullian, "Peter, whose interpreter[1] Mark was" (*Adv. Marc.* iv. 5). Jerome refers to "Mark, disciple and interpreter of Peter" (*de vir. illustr.* viii) and adds that Titus was Paul's interpreter. But Paul did not usually need an interpreter for he was fluent in Greek and Aramaic and probably knew Latin also.[2] Some think that Peter used Mark as his interpreter when he addressed audiences who understood Latin best. But this could have been quite seldom, for we have no account of Peter's work in North Africa or Spain where Latin would be most needed. Even in Rome Greek was current. "Simon Peter on the other hand, if he could express himself in Greek at all, could scarcely have possessed sufficient knowledge of the language to address a Roman congregation with success" (Swete, "Commentary," p. xx). This opinion hardly does justice to Peter's knowledge of the vernacular *Koine*. It is most likely

[1] Ἑρμηνευτής.

[2] Robertson, "Grammar of the Greek New Testament in the Light of Historical Research," p. 110.

that Peter spoke in Greek on the day of Pentecost since he addressed Jews from all parts of the world (Acts 2:9f., 14). Galilee was a bilingual country and most men needed to know both Aramaic and Greek. It is quite possible, however, that Peter did not feel at home in the Greek as in his native Aramaic, and even that had a Galilean accent (Matt. 26:73). Unless one has learned to think in a language and has an adequate vocabulary, he cannot speak rapidly and with ease before an audience. Swete ("Commentary," p. xix) notes that "when Joseph as an Egyptian prince communicates with his brethren from Palestine he uses the services of an interpreter."[1] And Paul forbids the exercise of the gift of tongues at Corinth unless an interpreter is present to translate what is said. Mark knew Aramaic well as a Jerusalem Jew and his Latin surname implies that he was a Hellenistic Jew on one side of his family and so would know Greek well. The Greek word for interpreter means "the secretary or dragoman who translates his master's words into a foreign tongue" (Swete,

[1] Cf. Gen. 42:23 (LXX) *ὁ γὰρ ἑρμηνευτὴς ἀνὰ μέσον αὐτῶν ἦν.*

"Commentary," p. xix). In our modern parlance Mark was Simon Peter's private secretary. He may indeed have been Peter's amanuensis for the First Epistle, though Peter seems to imply that Silvanus (Silas) performed that office on this occasion: "By Silvanus, our faithful brother, as I account him, I have written unto you briefly" (1 Pet. 5:12). We know that Tertius acted as amanuensis for Paul in the Epistle to the Romans (16:22). However, here Peter may mean that Silvanus simply acted as the bearer of the Epistle to the readers. In any case it is interesting to note that both Silas and Mark are here together with Peter, both former helpers of Paul. Evidently the old sore was healed long ago and everything was in good shape on all sides. If Peter wrote the Second Epistle, as I consider on the whole likely, it is possible that there we have a specimen of Peter's own Greek (quite vernacular), while in 1 Peter the amanuensis exercised certain liberties of style and statement.

5. The Genius for Personal Service.

Blessed is the man who finds the task for which he was made. It is not always easy to do. At school some pupils are drones in one class and stars in another. Others shine in every class. People have different turns beyond a doubt. The Holy Spirit bestows one gift upon one, another upon another (1 Cor. 12:11) "dividing to each one severally as he will." Undoubtedly Mark had a natural aptitude for personal service to those men whom he loved. "Not endowed with gifts of leadership, neither prophet nor teacher, he knew how to be invaluable to those who filled the first rank in the service of the Church, and proved himself a true *servus servorum Dei*" (Swete, "Commentary," pp. xv f.). He was "attendant" to Barnabas and Saul. He is now "interpreter" to Peter. He could make himself preëminently useful in such a relation. All arrangements for travel, provisions for food and lodging, carrying messages, arranging interviews, translating conversations or addresses, came natural to Mark. It was second nature to him and he enjoyed doing it. There is a story that Mark had once been a priest and that, after becoming a Christian, he amputated a finger so that he would be disqualified from being a priest any more.[1] It is hard to credit the story, though he may have had one stump-finger. But we are not to think of Mark as a mere valet to Barnabas, Paul, or Peter. It was not menial, but official service that he chiefly rendered, though he was ready to do any service that was necessary. He was the friend and companion of these great preachers, not a hireling. We have the words of Jesus for saying that the greatest in the Kingdom of God is he who serves most. Mark himself records it thus: "If any man would be first, he shall be last of all, and servant of all" (Mark 9:35). He also gives this logion of Jesus: "Whosoever would become great among you shall be your minister (servant); and whosoever would be first among you shall be servant (slave) of all" (Mark 10:44).[2] One may suppose that Peter told these sayings of Jesus and that Mark recorded them. They are pertinent words for Mark's own life. Humility is essential to real service. Peter wrote: "Yea, all of you gird yourselves with humility, to

[1] Hence the nickname *κολοβοδάκτυλος*.

[2] *διάκονος* and *δοῦλος*. Both used by Christ as terms of honor.

serve one another" (1 Pet. 5:5), doubtless with memories of the night when Jesus girded upon Himself the towel and washed the disciples' feet, even Peter's over his protest (John 13:5–11). Mark's own failure at Perga probably helped to make him humble now and able to sympathize more with the failings of others. Who can tell what is primary and what is secondary after all? It is not always true that the man most in the public eye is the one who does the greatest service for God and man. Jesus gave His estimate of His own work in terms of service. "For the Son of man also came not to be ministered unto, but to minister,[1] and to give his life a ransom for many" (Mark 10:45). Jesus glorified the little things of life and lifted the cup of cold water to the level of dignity and nobility. So we can understand the life of Florence Nightingale, of Clara Barton, of the Red Cross work, of the trained nurses of our time. We need waste no pity upon Mark because it fell to his lot to play second-fiddle, as we say, to great men like Paul, Barnabas, and Peter. Aaron was the mouthpiece of Moses. Luther had his Melancthon.

[1] *διακονῆσαι.*

The reward that one gets from God does not depend upon the post that he holds, but upon the fidelity with which the post is discharged. The minister is a steward of the mysteries of God and "it is required of stewards that a man be found faithful" (1 Cor. 4:2). Beyond a doubt Mark was happy with Peter and rejoiced in the favor that met Peter everywhere. Peter was the chief apostle of the twelve and Mark was the follower of this follower of Jesus. "Be ye imitators of me, even as I also am of Christ" (1 Cor. 11:1). So Paul openly taught. So Mark practised. He belonged to the second generation as did Paul, but Paul had a vision of Christ that made him an apostle as to one born out of due time (1 Cor. 15:8). There was, therefore, an inevitable discount in public opinion for one like Mark who companied with a man like Peter who had walked and talked with Jesus. Mark was a satellite and did nothing to throw a shadow in Peter's path. There was glory enough for both, as Schley said of the Santiago battle, but Peter was the man that men wished to hear. He spoke from personal acquaintance and intimate knowledge. The day was coming when there would be no more such men. Meanwhile it was their day and Mark did not begrudge Peter the post of honor at every turn. The rather he endeavored to make him comfortable and to make his message effective. If one is disposed to look down upon Mark for being willing to be a mere assistant to Peter, let him reflect that thus he enabled Peter to set forth Jesus to multitudes whom he could not otherwise reach. Peter's vivid Aramaic was transmuted into Mark's vivacious vernacular *Koine* and no doubt Mark took a certain pride in his skill as interpreter. In a sense he had to make the message his own and his own personality had a chance to count as he used his own turns of expression and favorite idioms. In serving Peter Mark was serving Christ. Mark widened the avenues of Peter's influence and Peter enlarged the sphere of Mark's activities. The two men supplemented each other. Mark was more than a Boswell to Peter, for in writing the Gospel the stamp of his own genius appears. That book is enough to immortalize any man, but that thought was furthest of all from Mark's mind. Peter taught Mark how to picture

Jesus so that men could see Him as he saw Him by the sea of Galilee. Who can say that the greatest achievement of Peter's life was not precisely this, that he so stamped the words and life of Jesus upon the mind of Mark, his interpreter and friend, that he was able to make that image the permanent possession of all the ages? It is hardly likely that Peter knew that his chief influence through the ages would be through John Mark. Our lives are strangely blended. The best that any one can do is to stand in his lot and to do his duty. Mark did his duty by Peter and Peter gave him his whole heart and loved him as a son. What cares the mother for all the myriad demands from her child? She joyfully gives all and gets all in the giving.

IX

MARK'S WONDROUS GOSPEL

"*Yea, I will give diligence that at every time ye may be able after my decease to call these things to remembrance.*"—2 PETER 1 : 15.

IX

MARK'S WONDROUS GOSPEL

1. The Purpose of Peter.

THE early writers differ very much in their views concerning the part that Peter played in the Gospel of Mark. This we shall examine presently. The point to note here is the possible, even probable, meaning of 2 Peter 1:15. There are difficulties, to be sure, in pressing this passage, since so many modern scholars deny the Petrine authorship of this Epistle. As for myself I hold with Bigg ("International Critical Commentary on 2 Peter") that the balance of probability is in favor of the Petrine authorship, though the arguments against it are admittedly strong. It is quite possible that in 2 Peter we have Peter's own somewhat uncouth vernacular *Koine* (cf. Acts 4:13) unrevised by Mark or Silas. On the basis of the genuineness of 2 Peter a very interesting question is raised by 1 : 15. What does Peter mean by giving diligence that after his decease[1] the readers of the Epistle may be able at every time to call these things to remembrance? What are "these things"? He uses the same expression in 1 : 12 and says that they "know them." He is speaking of the things of Christ and proceeds to affirm that he did not follow cunningly devised fables when he declared unto them "the power and coming of our Lord Jesus Christ, but we were eye-witnesses of his majesty" (2 Pet. 1 : 16). Then comes a reference to the glory on the Mount of Transfiguration. It seems a natural supposition and one that has won the support of various scholars[2] to-day that Peter has in mind a plan to have a Gospel prepared that shall put in permanent form his knowledge of Jesus. While he was "in this tabernacle" (1 : 13) he thought it his duty to put them in remembrance of the things of

[1] *ἔξοδον*. The word used of the death of Jesus in the talk with Moses and Elijah on the Mount (Luke 9 : 31).

[2] Irenæus (*Haer.* III. 1, 1) understands the passage to refer to Mark's Gospel, but misunderstands Peter as saying that the Gospel was to be written after his decease. He says that it is to be "written so as to be of use after his death" (Bigg, *in loco*).

Christ. It is a natural desire for one to wish to preserve what he knows so well for the benefit of those less favored. It is often one's duty to do this. Many, like Peter, find the burden of writing (*onus scribendi*) a fatal obstacle to authorship. It is not every gifted speaker who can, like Paul, wield the pen with equal facility. Spurgeon and Maclaren are modern instances of wizards alike with tongue and pen. But Peter was rich in the possession of one who had heard him preach so often that he understood perfectly his interpretation of Jesus. Besides, Mark, as Peter's interpreter, had already had long experience in this very thing. He was at home in the current vernacular *Koine* and would be able to do the literary side of the work more skillfully than Peter. On this view, then, Peter laid upon Mark the task of preparing his Memoirs of Jesus which Mark undertook as a filial trust. This is certainly a possible interpretation of 2 Peter 1 : 15. Bigg ("International Critical Commentary," *in loco*) says : "If a Gospel is meant, the reference can hardly be to any other than that of St. Mark."

2. The Suggestion of the Church at Rome.

Papias does not say that Peter proposed to Mark to write the Gospel nor does he say that the church at Rome made the suggestion. That is to say, Eusebius makes no quotation from Papias to that effect. But Eusebius (H. E. II. 15) does say on the authority of Papias and Clement of Alexandria that the Christians at Rome urged Mark to write the Gospel and that Peter approved it: "So charmed were the Romans with the light that shone in upon their minds from the discourses of Peter, that, not contented with a single hearing and the *viva voce* proclamation of the truth, they urged with the utmost solicitation on Mark, whose Gospel is in circulation and who was Peter's attendant, that he would leave them in writing a record of the teaching which they had received by word of mouth. They did not give over till they had prevailed on him: and thus they became the cause of the composition of the so-called Gospel according to Mark. It is said that when the apostle knew, by the revelation of the Spirit, what was done, he was pleased with the eagerness of the men and authorized the writing to be read in the churches" (Translation of J. H. Farmer in International Standard Bible Encyclopædia). The account given by Clement of Alexandria (Hypotyp. as quoted in Eusebius, H. E. VI. 14) is quite similar: "The occasion for writing the Gospel according to Mark was as follows: After Peter had publicly preached the word in Rome and declared the Gospel by the Spirit, many who were present entreated Mark, as one who had followed him for a long time and remembered what he said, to write down what he had spoken, and Mark, after composing the Gospel, presented it to his petitioners. When Peter became aware of it, he neither eagerly hindered nor promoted it" (*ibid.*). We thus seem to have a definite and fairly certain tradition that connects our Gospel of Mark with Rome. Clement of Alexandria wrote about 200 A. D. The work was done also while Peter was alive. Eusebius (H. E. V. 8), however, quotes Irenæus (*Adv. Haer.* III. 1) as saying that "after the departure" (exit, "exodus") of Paul and Peter, Mark, Peter's disciple, delivered to us in writing the things preached by Peter. Irenæus apparently locates the writing in Rome, but after Peter's death. It is not possible to tell who is right as to the time except by an appeal to synoptic criticism. That decides against Irenæus. However, Mark's Gospel is generally called the Roman Gospel since it apparently made its appearance in Rome and suits the Roman love of action and power. It has even been suggested that Mark wrote his Gospel in Latin, but this is pure conjecture.

3. Early Date of Mark's Gospel.

It is here assumed against Blass, Marshall, and Wellhausen that Mark wrote his Gospel, not in Aramaic, but in Greek. Swete ("Commentary," p. xxxvii) observes that the use of both transliteration and translation of Aramaic terms by Mark shows that he is not translating, but writing freely in Greek. It is assumed also that the present canonical Gospel is substantially as Mark wrote it. There may have been a few editorial touches here and there, but not many. Hawkins, after an elaborate and minute examination of the peculiarities of Mark's Gospel, admits some eight or ten verbal additions ("Horæ Synopticæ," p. 152). But the essential unity of the book is proven. Swete sums the matter up thus: "The present writer has risen from his study of the Gospel with a strong sense of the unity of the work, and can echo the *requiescat Urmarkus* which ends a recent discussion" ("Commentary," pp. 1 f., note). Minor editorial revision is quite a different matter from the theory of Bacon that a Redactor reworked Mark's original Gospel and produced our present canonical Gospel under Pauline influences ("Beginnings of Gospel Story," pp. xvii–xxxiii). Another modern theory is that of Wendling[1] who finds three Marks (M^1, M^2, M^3). The last is our canonical Mark. The first he calls the historian, the second the poet, the third the theologian. It is all very pretty and very improbable. Holdsworth ("Gospel Origins," p. 115) thinks that Mark himself made three editions of his Gospel (one in Cæsarea, one in Alexandria, and one in Rome (our Gospel). But all this speculation clears away when we face the fact that our present Gospel of Mark must in all probability itself be dated in the fifties. It is now a commonplace in synoptic criticism that

[1] "Urmarcus," 1905; "Die Entstehung des Marcusevangeliums," 1909.

Mark's Gospel was used by Matthew and Luke. "The most notable achievement in the department of recent New Testament criticism is undoubtedly the fairly general agreement arrived at with regard to the mutual relations of the first three Gospels" (M. Jones, "The New Testament in the Twentieth Century," 1914, p. 189). "The priority of St. Mark's Gospel is now generally accepted by modern critics" (Holdsworth, "Gospel Origins," 1913, p. 104). This is the fact as scholars to-day view it. John's Gospel is the latest and was written to supplement the Synoptic Gospels. It is not clear whether Luke made use of Matthew or not, but certainly Luke wrote his Gospel before the Acts, for he refers to it in Acts 1 : 1. The probable explanation of the close of the Acts with Paul a prisoner in Rome for two years is that Luke wrote the Acts during those two years and closed the book at that point because events had only developed that far. Harnack (" Date of the Acts and the Synoptic Gospels," tr. 1911, p. 99) holds that the concluding verses of Acts "make it in the highest degree probable that the work was written at a time when St. Paul's trial in Rome had not yet come to an end." It must come before the destruction of Jerusalem and the death of Paul (*ibid.*, p. 116), before the burning of Rome, and probably in the year A. D. 62 (*ibid.*, p. 92). This position compels us to place the date of Luke's Gospel before A. D. 62, and we must date it either in the early part of Paul's first Roman imprisonment (A. D. 59 or 60) or, as is most likely, the close of the imprisonment in Cæsarea (A. D. 58 or 59). Now Luke made use of both oral and written sources in preparing his Gospel (Luke 1 : 1–4). The body of Mark's Gospel is reproduced in both Matthew and Luke as any one can see for himself by looking at a Harmony of the Gospels like that of Broadus or of Stevens and Burton. Clearly then Mark's Gospel is earlier than the Gospel of Luke (and of Matthew). But how much earlier? If Luke made use of Matthew also, we should have to place the Greek Matthew about A. D. 54 to 57. But that is not certain. But in any case there is every probability that Mark's Gospel in Greek appeared in the early years of the fifth decade[1] (A. D. 50 to 55). At first this conclusion may seem

[1] Nolloth, "The Rise of the Christian Religion," 1917, p. 19.

inconsistent with the tradition that Mark's Gospel was written in Rome. There is, however, nothing to make it so. Peter and Mark could very well have been in Rome in the early fifties and then again at the time of the writing of 1 Peter 5 : 13. It is shown therefore that Mark's Gospel is the earliest of our canonical Gospels and is the historical framework of both Matthew and Luke. It is impossible, therefore, to overestimate the importance of this earliest Gospel to the modern student. "No man can pretend to have seriously examined the historical basis of the Christian faith who has not to some extent applied the ordinary processes of historical criticism to the Gospel of Mark, the earliest extant embodiment of the evangelic story" (Bacon, "The Beginnings of the Gospel Story," 1909, p. vii). Even Pfleiderer is willing to admit: "Nothing can be urged against the church tradition that this Gospel was written by John Mark" ("Christian Origins," tr. 1906, p. 222), the John Mark who left Paul and Barnabas at Perga, but who has "come back" in great form in his work with Simon Peter. Thank God that a young preacher can rise above a blunder and make good in another place after failure.

4. **Peter's Reminiscences.**

There is nothing in the book itself that would prove that Mark obtained his information chiefly from Simon Peter. But, once this fact is admitted, there is abundant illustration and confirmation of its correctness. Papias says that Mark became the interpreter of Peter, and "whatever he remembered,[1] he wrote accurately, not however in order, the things either said or done by Christ." Papias adds that Peter "made his instructions to meet the needs (of his hearers, like other preachers), but not as if he were making an orderly arrangement[2] (or full report) of the Lord's discourses.[3] So then Mark made no mistake writing thus some things as he recalled[4] them, for he took forethought for one thing, to omit nothing of what he had heard and to make no false statement in them." Papias, as quoted in Eusebius, has here given a very modest picture of Mark's Gospel and

[1] *ἐμνημόνευσεν*. [2] *σύνταξιν*.

[3] *τῶν κυριακῶν λογίων*. Cf. the recently discovered *Logia of Jesus* by Grenfell and Hunt (1897); "New Sayings of Jesus" (1904). [4] *ἀπεμνημόνευσεν*.

yet one wholly in accord with the book as we have it. It is not a complete story of the life of Jesus. All the early life and most of the early ministry is passed by. It is quite incomplete, but it is accurate and, in the main, chronological. Justin Martyr (*Dial. with Trypho*, cvi) calls this Gospel Peter's "Memoirs,"[1] or Memorabilia like Xenophon's Memorabilia of Socrates. Irenæus (*Adv. Haer.* III. 1) says that Mark "has delivered to us in writing the things preached by Peter." Tertullian (*Adv. Marc.*, IV. 5) says that this Gospel "may be ascribed to Peter, whose interpreter Mark was." Origen in his commentary on Matthew (Eus. H. E. VI. 25) states that Mark "composed it as Peter guided him,[2] who therefore in his Catholic epistle acknowledged the evangelist as his son." Eusebius (*Dem. Evang.* III. 5) expressly says: "Mark indeed writes this, but it is Peter who so testifies about himself, for all that is in Mark are memoirs of the discourses of Peter." Jerome *De vir. illustr.*, XI.) has carried this tradition still further: "whose Gospel was composed, Peter narrating and Mark writing."

[1] Ἀπομνημονεύματα.

[2] ὡς Πέτρος ὑφηγήσατο αὐτῷ.

Evidently the story of Peter's connection with Mark's Gospel grew through the centuries from Papias (about A. D. 125) to Jerome (about A. D. 350). We may drop at once the notion that Peter dictated the second Gospel and that Mark was merely his amanuensis or even that Peter "guided" Mark in the composition (Origen), though that is less unlikely. We may admit as probable that Peter saw the book and approved its use as Clement of Alexandria states, who says that Peter was pleased with the eagerness of the Roman Christians about the Gospel "and authorized the writing to be read in the churches" (Eus. H. E. II. 15). But what seems indisputable is the fact that Mark used his recollections of Peter's preaching as the chief basis of the book. He heard Peter a great deal for a number of years. He probably made notes in Aramaic or in Greek of Peter's preaching. Nolloth ("The Rise of the Christian Religion," p. 23) even thinks that Matthew made notes of Christ's preaching during His ministry in Aramaic and that this was the origin of the Logia of Jesus (the Q of criticism). He speaks also of "the Aramaic notes of the preaching of St. Peter made by his 'interpreter' St.

Mark, forming the original copy of the Second Gospel." Thus the two oldest sources of the life of Jesus go back to the apostles Matthew and Peter. It is, therefore, quite proper to say that Peter's Reminiscences of Jesus are preserved in the Gospel of Mark. The book is in a true sense the Memoirs or Memorabilia of Peter.

If now we turn to Mark's Gospel we shall find many things that corroborate this position. The book reveals many tokens of an eye-witness and some of these come most naturally from Simon Peter. The abundant use of the historical present in Mark's Gospel is probably due to Peter's lively descriptive powers. He pictured the incidents so clearly that Mark saw them as actually going on and so narrated them as doubtless Peter told them. There are 151 historic presents in Mark and only 78 in Matthew, though a much longer book, only 6 in Luke and 13 in Acts.[1] This list does not include parables for Mark has no historic presents in them. Mark is very fond of the imperfect tense which is another way of using Peter's eyes and Peter's imagination. There are numerous details

[1] Hawkins, "Horæ Synopticæ," pp. 147 ff.

which also confirm this theory, a few of which are here given. When Jesus healed Peter's mother-in-law we read that "he came and took her by the hand and raised her up" (Mark 1:31). At even we find that "all the city was gathered at the door" (1:33), the description probably of Peter who stood in the door of his home with Jesus and watched the excited throng pass by as they were healed. It seems to be Peter also who gives this life-like touch: "And in the morning, a great while before day, he rose up and went out (probably Peter heard him go), and departed into a desert place, and there prayed. And Simon and they that were with him followed after him (rushed[1] after him in eager pursuit); and they found him, and say unto him, All men are seeking thee" (1:35–37). Mark's narrative here bears every trace of Peter's excitement and impetuosity and vivid imagination in description. In 2:2 we read that "there was no longer room *for them*, no, not even about the door." Jesus was here "at home"[2] or "indoors" (2:1) as we say, preserving Peter's colloquial reference to his

[1] *κατεδίωξεν*. Perfective use of *κατά*.
[2] *ἐν οἴκῳ*. Some manuscripts *εἰς οἶκον*.

own house in Capernaum. Mark has much about the feelings and looks of Jesus (cf. 1:43; 3:5; 5:32; 6:40) which come naturally from an eye-witness. "Certainly no amount of realism will account for the scores of unexpected and independent details with which St. Mark enriches the common narrative" (Swete, "Commentary," p. lvii). Suffice it to mention one other touch of life. In 6:39f. Mark speaks of the "green" grass and notes that they were grouped "in companies"[1] like guests at a banquet (*symposia*) and that their many-colored garments on the green grass in the afternoon sun made them look like "garden-beds"[2] ("in ranks"). There are literally hundreds of such vivid details in Mark, some of which are preserved in Matthew and Luke, but most of which are smoothed away in their more literary arrangement. Mark's Gospel is, like that of John, full of animation, of dialogue, of pictures. It is to the credit of Mark that, though he may not have heard Jesus himself, yet he has faithfully preserved the word-pictures of Peter who did hear Christ preach and saw Him do

[1] *συμπόσια συμπόσια.*

[2] *πρασιαὶ πρασιαί.* Nominative absolute.

His work. Peter described Jesus to Cornelius as one "who went about doing good, and healing all that were oppressed of the devil; for God was with him" (Acts 10:38). Mark, as we have seen, may have been of the six brethren with Peter in Cæsarea and may thus have heard Peter say these words. At any rate they give an adequate conception of Mark's own Gospel, which is, at bottom, Peter's Gospel.

5. Other Sources Used by Mark.

There is no reason to think that Mark confined himself to what he heard from Peter. He, like Luke (1:1–4), had heard other "eye-witnesses"[1] of the Lord tell their story at his mother's home in Jerusalem and elsewhere. There are portions of Mark's Gospel that do not come naturally from Peter. If Luke (1:1–4) employed on a large scale the methods of the historian in making his researches, why may not Mark have done so on a smaller scale? It is probable that the so-called Logia of Jesus (Q), whether written by Matthew in Aramaic as Papias says or by some one else, was earlier than Mark.

[1] αὐτόπται.

Ramsay (*The Expositor*, May, 1907) suggests that Q was written during the lifetime of Jesus. Salmon ("The Human Element in the Gospels," p. 274) takes the same view. At any rate it is probable that Q is older than Mark. It is even held by some that Mark made use of Q to some extent.[1] There is nothing impossible or even improbable in a limited use of Q by Mark. The objection to an extended use is precisely the vivid power of most of the book which bears the stamp of Peter's burning story. Chapter 13 is called "The Little Apocalypse" and may represent another source used by Mark. It may have been a written source (Swete, "Commentary," p. lix) because in 13:14 the words "Let him that readeth understand"[2] would imply that, provided they belonged to the source. We know from Luke 1:1–4 that "many" undertook to tell their story about various aspects of the words and deeds of Jesus. Mark wrote with freedom and concern at the same time to be faithful to the data in hand. Swete properly sums up the

[1] Cf. Streeter, "St. Mark's Knowledge and Use of Q" ("Oxford Studies in the Synoptic Problem"), 1911, pp. 165–183.

[2] ὁ ἀναγινώσκων νοείτω.

matter thus: "On the whole it seems safe to assume as a working theory of the origination of the Gospel that its main source is the teaching of St. Peter, which has supplied nearly the entire series of notes descriptive of the Galilean Ministry, and has largely influenced the remainder of the book" ("Commentary," p. lix).

6. The Close of the Gospel.

It seems certain that Mark did not close his Gospel as we have it in our New Testaments. The two oldest and best Greek manuscripts of the New Testament (Aleph or Codex Sinaiticus and B or Codex Vaticanus) close with verse 8 of chapter 16 and with the words, "for they were afraid." At first one has a shock of surprise to find such an ending. Maclean (Hastings' Dictionary of Christ and the Gospels) considers it "inconceivable" that this "abrupt and inauspicious" ending can be the way that Mark closed his book. But Farmer (International Standard Bible Encyclopædia) thinks that "it is just possible that the Gospel did end at verse 8. The very abruptness would argue an early date when Christians lived in the atmosphere of the Resurrection and would form an even appropriate closing for the Gospel of the Servant." So the doctors disagree very widely. It is possible that Mark did not end his Gospel here. The real ending may have been lost. The last leaf of the roll may have been lost very early. "I regard it nevertheless as one of the possibilities of future finds that we receive this Gospel with its own authentic finish. Mark has been connected with Alexandria. May Grenfell and Hunt add to their numerous gifts the close of the original Mark from an Egyptian papyrus" (Gregory, "The Canon and Text of the New Testament," 1907, p. 512). The present long ending has been ascribed to Ariston, probably the Aristion mentioned in Papias, by an Armenian scribe who wrote in between verses 8 and 9 in red ink the words "*Ariston Eredzou*" (Ariston the Presbyter). This discovery was made by Mr. F. C. Conybeare. "So here at last was the missing evidence for the last twelve verses, and a discovery for critical confirmation which should be the end of all strife" (Rendel Harris, "Sidelights on New Testament Research," 1908, p. 92).

Several Greek manuscripts (L and three other uncials and four cursives) have two endings, the usual one and a shorter one, while the Old Latin K has only the short one. It reads as follows: "All that had been commanded to them they briefly reported to Peter and his company. And after this Jesus Himself appeared to them and from the east even unto the west sent forth by them the holy and incorruptible proclamation of the eternal salvation." No one defends this ending which is an evident makeshift to supply a suitable close for the Gospel of Mark.

The newly-discovered Washington Manuscript (W), itself as old as Aleph and B and kept in this country, has an expanded ending. After verse 14 of the usual long ending we find these words: "And they defended themselves saying that this age of lawlessness and sin is under the power of Satan, who, through unclean spirits, does not suffer the true virtue of God to be apprehended. Therefore now reveal Thy righteousness. And Christ addressed them and said, 'The limit of the years of the authority of Satan has been reached, but other dread things are coming: and it was for those who had sinned that I was delivered to death that they might return to the Truth and sin no more, but inherit the spiritual and immortal glory of righteousness in heaven'" (Rendel Harris' translation, "Side-lights on New Testament Research," p. 90).[1] Then the usual ending proceeds. These various endings throw suspicion upon one another and we can only say that we do not now know how Mark ended his Gospel. Some day we may know.

7. **Characteristics of Mark's Gospel.**

The Gospel of Mark did not at first rank as high as the other Gospels. Two (Matthew and John) were by apostles themselves, while Mark was only a disciple of an apostle. Luke's Gospel is much longer and has greater literary charm. Mark's is the briefest and was slighted by many. The earliest commentary that is preserved is ascribed to Victor of Antioch (fifth or sixth century) who says that he knew of none on Mark's Gospel.

[1] Cf. also Cobern, "The New Archæological Discoveries and Their Bearing Upon the New Testament," 1917, p. 164.

The book had no settled place in the manuscripts, sometimes coming last of the Four Gospels as in the Washington Manuscript. The early writers varied greatly in the symbol for Mark, using each of the four for him (lion, man, ox, eagle). But all this is changed now and the merit of this Gospel is better appreciated. "It is seen, too, to be at the basis of the whole problem of the mutual relations of the canonical Gospels, and is believed by many to take us nearest the primitive form of the evangelical narrative. So it has become the subject of a quite peculiar interest, and engages the sedulous attention of students" (Salmond, Hastings' Dictionary of the Bible).

It is clear that Mark wrote out his recollections of Peter's preaching *con amore.* There was an affinity between the minds of the two men. Each had a lively style, direct, simple, objective, picturesque, telling, and realistic. No doubt Peter had influenced Mark's style unconsciously. Both Peter and Mark were impulsive and warm-hearted. Each made mistakes and each rallied and did his real work afterwards. Peter denied his Lord (a great sin) and Mark deserted his leader (a great blunder). The stamp of Peter's mind is upon this Gospel, but Mark's hand is in it also. The book seems like a torso without beginning or proper ending. It is a mere sketch, but it has a powerful grasp of the heart of Christ's life. It is a book of action and power, but the words of Jesus are not neglected. The miracles are more prominent than the parables, but the teaching of Jesus is in evidence. We see Christ the Preacher and the Teacher in Mark as well as Christ the Healer and the Saviour from sin. There is little discussion of doctrine, but the Cross is central in the book and the Atonement is stated in the words of Jesus who came "to give his life a ransom for many" (10:45). There is the graphic style of an eye-witness with the sure swiftness of a cinema machine. Jesus is here drawn to the life. And Jesus is the center of everything in this book. "In addition to all this evidence there is the oft-recurring reference to the lights and shadows that passed over the Face of Jesus in joy and sorrow, satisfaction and disappointment, indignation and anger" (Luckock, "The Special Characteristics of the Four Gospels," 1900,

p. 93). Peter pictured Christ so that the picture set Mark's mind all ablaze with interest and enthusiasm. Christian artists have painted Peter holding a book and Mark a pen or Peter preaching while Mark is taking notes. That is an exaggerated portrayal of Peter's influence on Mark who certainly retained his own individuality in the work.

It is often said that John's Gospel sets forth the Deity of Christ[1] while the Gospel of Mark presents His Humanity.[2] That is true in a general way, but the Humanity of Jesus is in the Gospel of John and the Deity of Jesus in the Gospel of Mark. It is there by implication and by statement. Pfleiderer sees this clearly. "This oldest Evangelist furnishes the truest impression which Jesus made on His environment,—here He actually lives and works" ("Christian Origins," p. 219). And yet Pfleiderer has to add: "He wrote for Heathen-Christians and wished to awaken or confirm the conviction that, despite the rejection by the Jews, Jesus of Nazareth was

[1] Cf. my "Divinity of Christ in the Gospel of John" (1916).

[2] Cf. "The Humanity of Jesus Christ" (pp. 105–114 of Luckock's "Characteristics of the Four Gospels").

proven to be the Christ and the Son of God by wonders and signs of every kind." That is true, little as Pfleiderer likes it. The Christ of Mark's Gospel is in reality the Christ of Peter, of John, of Matthew, of Luke, of Paul, of them all, Son of God and Son of man, Lord and Saviour of men.

Mark's Gospel is consummate art after all without meaning to be art at all, "a work wherein the artist is more completely effaced by his subject" (Von Soden, "Early Christian Literature," tr. 1906, p. 153). One never thinks of Mark in reading his Gospel, but one sees Jesus, hears Him, loves Him, follows Him, worships Him.

X

WINNING PAUL'S PRAISE

"*And Mark, the cousin of Barnabas (touching whom ye received commandment; if he come unto you, receive him*)."—COL. 4:10.

"*Take Mark, and bring him with thee; for he is useful to me for ministering.*"—2 TIM. 4:11.

X

WINNING PAUL'S PRAISE

1. Co-Worker With Paul in Rome.

TIME heals many sores, time and work and the grace of God. Some fifteen years have passed since Mark deserted Paul at Perga and ten or a dozen since the fatal breach at Antioch between Paul and Barnabas over Mark (Acts 15:39). Paul has evidently watched the career of Mark with genuine interest and is now glad to see that he was mistaken in his opinion of the essential fickleness of Mark's character. Mark has proven by his work with Barnabas and with Peter that the root of the matter is in him. The result is that he has wholly recovered Paul's good opinion. Barnabas and Peter have had him in tow and they have done their work well. It used to be the fashion for old preachers to take young preachers through a course of "swamp theology" and practical experience. The young preacher would read theology with a master just as a young lawyer would read law under a great jurist and a young physician would read medicine with a great practitioner. There were some advantages in such a practical and personal clinic, but it takes a great deal of time and may be a rather narrow and one sided discipline. Schools do better on the whole for most men and yet it must be admitted that Mark reflects credit on his teachers in the end of the day. It is possible that Peter is also in Rome at this time with Paul and Mark, though the probability is rather against it since he could hardly be omitted from the list of Paul's Jewish co-workers in Rome, for he says "these only" in Colossians 4:11. Probably Peter left Rome before Paul came and Mark remained. It is generally thought that Barnabas was now dead, since Mark is with Paul. But this is a "somewhat precarious" argument (Lightfoot, Col. *in loco*). Paul is affectionate in his reference to Barnabas here and in 1 Corinthians 9:6. There was no sting left by the clash at Antioch in Galatians 2:11 ff. and the subsequent separation (Acts 15:39). Great souls can forgive a wrong and drop a quarrel even if they do not literally forget the episode. They do not cherish it. They let bygones be bygones.

It is good to see Mark with Paul once more. Surely Mark felt grateful at this clinching evidence that Paul now looked with affection and satisfaction upon the young man who went not to the work (Acts 15:38). He was no longer "Mark the Apostate" as Paul had branded him with a word that burned through the years. He is actually one of Paul's "co-workers" or "fellow-workers[1] unto the Kingdom of God." He is no longer a mere "attendant" doing personal service, but is ranked with the best and most faithful of Paul's helpers in Rome. Paul notes a group of these Jewish Christians in Rome who are loyal to him (Aristarchus, Mark, Jesus Justus) and "these only."[2] We know from Philippians 1:15–18 that some of the Jewish Christians in Rome took pleasure in annoying Paul out of envy and strife, probably Judaizers who have come on to Rome.[3] Paul's language here need not be

[1] *συνεργοὶ εἰς τὴν βασιλείαν τοῦ θεοῦ.*
[2] *οὗτοι μόνοι.*
[3] Cf. Lightfoot, Philippians, *in loco.*

pressed too literally, but certainly it means that among the prominent Jewish Christians in Rome Paul can name these three alone as men on whom he can count in the present emergency (Lightfoot, *in loco*). In Philippians 2:20f. Paul again notes how all except Timothy "seek their own, not the things of Christ." Mark now has an honorable place in this small list of Pauline loyalists. He is no longer a deserter, but one to be trusted.

These are "men that have been a comfort unto me"[1] (Col. 4:11). The word here for "comfort" occurs nowhere else in the New Testament. The range of meaning is wider than the commoner words, but the medical use for assuaging or alleviating pain comes to be the predominant one. Once Mark because of his defection was a spiritual irritant to Paul and it was disturbing to have him with him. Now his presence is soothing and cheering to Paul the prisoner. Clearly Mark is taking pains to be pleasing and helpful to Paul and he has succeeded. There is a wonderful difference in people about this matter

[1] οἵτινες ἐγενήθησάν μοι παρηγορία. The technical use of παρηγορία is medical (our paregoric).

of consolation. It pays the pastor to study calmness and gentleness of manner so that his presence may leave the sick better and not worse. It does make a difference whether the fur is rubbed the wrong way. Probably Paul made a point of letting Mark know that he acknowledged his error of judgment about him and expressed pleasure in his achievements. Kind words cost little, but they go far toward smoothing the path of weary toilers who have many unknown causes for annoyance.

But the crowning word of praise from Paul occurs in 2 Tim. 4 : 11 where he says of Mark: "for he is useful to me for ministering."[1] Once Mark was useless to Paul and he stoutly refused to take him along with him on the second mission tour because of his failure in the first. Now Paul explains to Timothy why he wants him and puts the verb first as if to say: "He *is* useful to me." He has made good with Paul in great style right where he was weak. Surely Timothy told Mark these words of Paul, words that would warm the cockles of his heart and make him

[1] *ἔστιν γάρ μοι εὔχρηστος εἰς διακονίαν.* The position and accent of *ἔστιν* emphasizes the point.

happy. The reason for mentioning this passage here is that Paul is manifestly alluding to what Mark did for him before the second Roman imprisonment. It is a backward glance at Mark's previous service to Paul. The allusion seems to be to the time of Colossians 4:10, when Mark was with Paul in Rome. We do not know to what Paul refers by the general expression "useful for ministering." White suggests that, since Mark was Peter's interpreter of Aramaic into Greek, so here he is Paul's interpreter of Greek into Latin (Expositor's Greek Testament, *in loco*). This is, of course, possible. Paul probably knew Latin, but may not have been fluent in it and he may have had some need for Latin converse in his dealings with the Prætorian Guard (Phil. 1:13) or with Cæsar's household (Phil. 4:22). Others have suggested that Paul read Mark's Gospel while in Rome and that it may have been included in Paul's list of books that he left at Troas (2 Tim. 4:13). This also is quite possible. Some critics imagine that they can detect a Pauline influence in Mark's Gospel. Paul may have acknowledged a contribution from Mark to his own intellectual and spiritual life.

Whatever the service was Paul sincerely appreciated it and confessed himself debtor to Mark his co-worker, comfort, and helper. Praise like this from Paul would compensate Mark for much that he had suffered and was rich reward for the years of sincere endeavor to make his life tell for Christ.

2. Commended by Paul to the Colossians.

Mark apparently means to make a visit to Colossæ, for Paul says: "If he come unto you, receive him" (Col. 4 : 10). He may have had an engagement with Peter in this region. It seems likely that this visit was made, for Mark sends a salutation to the saints of Asia and the other Roman provinces when Peter writes to them (1 Pet. 5 : 13). It is probable that Paul's former poor opinion of Mark had spread over a wide area since he took so much trouble now to correct it (Maclean, Hastings' Dictionary of Christ and the Gospels). "The Pauline churches, which were aware of the estrangement, might not be very ready to give a hearty welcome to Mark" (Gould, "International Critical Commentary," *in loco*). Paul is evidently anxious to remove any remaining prejudice against Mark so that he may be able to do well what he has to perform. Paul had written the Colossians before on the subject of Mark's reception, "touching whom ye received commandments"[1] (Col. 4 : 10). The "commandments" in question could have been sent by word of mouth or by letter. If not by letter, Lightfoot suggests Peter or Barnabas as the bearer of Paul's message about Mark. One of the "commandments" Paul repeats: "If he come unto you, receive[2] him." The word "receive" was the usual term for hospitable welcome.[3] Paul is now willing to underwrite Mark before he comes to Colossæ. It is not a case of Paul's being anxious to get rid of Mark. People sometimes write the most enthusiastic letters of commendation of those whom they wish to palm off upon somebody else. Paul is not trying to victimize the Colossians. It is now precisely because he has found Mark "useful" and "a comfort" that he is so glad to speak a good word about him to the church in Colossæ. That is a useful and a kind

[1] *περὶ οὗ ἐλάβετε ἐντολάς*. The epistolary aorist is ruled out here (Lightfoot).

[2] *δέξασθε*.

[3] In Luke 10 : 38 we have *Μάρθα ὑπεδέξατο αὐτόν*.

thing to do. Peripatetic preachers have been known to take advantage of such particular commendation. One should be sure of his man before he gives him a *carte blanche* letter of endorsement. Paul cared little for such matters and ridiculed the Judaizers who went to Corinth with genuine or spurious letters of recommendation to influence the brethren: "Or need we, as do some, epistles of commendation to you or from you" (2 Cor. 3:1). Paul is not giving this note of commendation to Mark, but to the Colossians about him. It is certain that, when Mark came to Colossæ, he found a kindly spirit toward him. Paul knew what it was to have a man like Barnabas stand voucher for him when he was under suspicion.

3. In His Old Haunts in the East.

We know that Mark went east again, because in 2 Timothy 4:11 Paul urges Timothy, when in Ephesus, to "take[1] Mark, and bring him." "It is implied that Mark was somewhere on the line of route between Ephesus and Rome, but we do not know

[1] ἀναλαβὼν. Vulgate *assume*. Cf. also Acts 20:13, 14; 23:31. They "picked up Paul" at Assos. In 23:31 we have ἀναλαβόντες ἤγαγον as here (ἄγε).

the precise place" (White, Expositor's Greek Testament, *in loco*). It was probably at Colossæ or Miletus. Mark was now an expert workman and no novice. He no longer had need to be ashamed of his work nor was Paul ashamed of it (2 Tim. 2:15). The rather Paul was now proud of his old protégé. It is amazing how much a young preacher can develop with the years. "Be diligent in these things; give thyself wholly to them; that thy progress[1] may be manifest unto all" (1 Tim. 4:15). Mark had now forged his way to the front so that all men could see. He had very distinctly "arrived." Once a young preacher, just starting to college, innocently enough impressed a deacon that he was too "fast" for a preacher because he rode a plow-horse all sorts of gaits. The deacon was very positive in his judgment and free with his criticism. Years later he wrote to the preacher a letter of apology, but added that no young preacher ought ever to be discouraged since God had done what he had with this victim of the deacon's prejudice. He was entirely right. No man should be disheartened by difficulties or by

[1] *Προκοπή* cutting ahead.

adverse criticism. It is far better to surmount the obstacles and to turn them to glorious gain. Mark is now out from under the cloud of reproach. He had long ago "vindicated and justified the risk Barnabas had run in giving him a chance of recovering his character" (White, Expositor's Greek Testament, *in loco*).

4. Longed for by the Lonely Paul.

Paul had once scouted the proposal of Barnabas to "take along" John Mark. But now he hungers for the comfort of his presence. During his former imprisonment in Rome Paul had learned to lean on Mark as a reliable staff. Now he is in prison again with no liberties and fewer friends. He has no hired house to which they can come. He is probably in the dread Mamertine dungeon and few, like Onesiphorus, have the courage to make diligent search to find the old Lion of Liberty and to face death for his sake (2 Tim. 1 : 17). One by one Paul's co-workers left him on one pretext or another. "Demas forsook me, having loved this present world, and went to Thessalonica; Crescens to Galatia, Titus to Dalmatia" (2 Tim. 4 : 10). So the melancholy record runs. It is like a wholesale Perga, only they all gave "the work" as the reason for leaving Paul to his fate which all foresaw. It is pathetic beyond words as the aged prisoner goes on to add in his cold and dreariness: "Only Luke is with me." Blessings on this "beloved physician" who is not afraid of death and who risks his own life for the sake of his great friend. This is one of the great friendships of history, that between Paul and Luke. It is fitting for the preacher and the physician to be fast friends. They both deal with the realities of life and see people in their hours of weakness and of need. They ought to work together in harmony. The physician ought to be a Christian. It is a pity to see the preacher the tool of a quack. Paul and Luke were both men of genius, of culture, of passion for Christ and for humanity. But, much as Luke is to Paul, his heart goes out after two young preachers who have meant much to him. He wants them to be by his side when the end comes, as he knows it will come soon. One of these is Timothy, of course. It seems that Timothy did come and was put in prison for his courageous stand by Paul. In Hebrews 13:23 we read: "Know ye that our brother Timothy hath been set at liberty." The other young preacher, young in comparison with "Paul the aged," is Mark. "Take Mark, and bring him with thee; for he is useful to me for ministering." As the shadows close round us, we wish only real friends about us, real friends and real books. So Sir Walter Scott died with his loved ones about him who brought him "The Book," the only Book to live by and to die by. Paul longs for Timothy and Mark and his "cloak" and "the books, especially the parchments." Precious books were these, perhaps with marginal comments by Paul. Some of them were probably parts of the Old Testament in Hebrew or in Greek. One of them may have been Luke's Gospel, another the Acts, another may have been Mark's Gospel. Paul means to keep up his "ministry" to the end. "But I hold not my life of any account as dear unto myself, so that I may accomplish my course, and the ministry which I received from the Lord Jesus, to testify the gospel of the grace of God" (Acts 20:24). So Paul spoke to the elders of Ephesus at Miletus nearly a dozen years before. His ministry is near its close, but he will keep on to the very end. So he wants Mark "for ministering." Mark had shown a genius for helping great men and now the last wish of Paul is that Mark may be at his side to help him make the last days full of service for Christ. We may be sure that Mark came if it lay in his power to do so. We may think, therefore, of Luke, Timothy and Mark, together with some of the brave spirits in Rome, as the faithful band that saw the greatest preacher of the ages pay the price of loyalty to Jesus Christ with his own life.

This is a good place to leave Mark. Here we must leave him, for our sources of information all fail us. Mark kept to the path of service to the end, we may be sure. He was not a genius on the scale of Paul or of John. He apparently lacked the gifts of oratory possessed by Barnabas and Peter. But he learned to make himself useful to others and to make the most of the talents that he had. He became "a good minister of Christ Jesus" (1 Tim. 4:6). That is a nobler achievement than merely spectacular gifts that are not wisely used. That goal is possible to us all. Mark should be an inspiration to the average minister who has to toil in obscure places and unrecognized by the great majority and who makes mistakes that dishearten him. It is all a part of the day's work. Preachers are made out of men, out of the same human stuff that other people have. Preachers are made out of laymen. Give us better laymen and we shall have better preachers. But preachers are entitled to more than one chance. We should magnify our office and magnify Christ. In the end what matters most is that we did an honest day's work. People have their tastes about preaching as about everything else. In Scotland, that land of good preaching, there are "sermon-tasters" who know how to sample sermons by the smack of the words. We know very little after all about the respective merits of preachers. "Wherefore judge nothing before the time, until the Lord come, who will bring to light the hidden things of darkness, and make manifest the counsels of the heart; and then shall each man have his praise from God" (1 Cor. 4:5). And Mark now has "the praise" from God which is better even than that from Paul.

Special Books on Mark and His Gospel

(*Apart from continuous commentaries by the same author, books on all the Gospels, the Synoptic problem, Cyclopædia articles.*)

Abbott, E. A., The Fourfold Gospel (Diatessarica, Sections III, IV, V, 1915, 1916, 1917. These three volumes are devoted to Mark).

Alexander, Gospel according to St. Mark. 1863.

Allen, The Gospel according to Mark. 1915.

Bacon, The Beginnings of Gospel Story: A Historico-Critical Inquiry into the Sources of and Structure of the Gospel according to Mark. 1909.

Badham, St. Mark's Indebtedness to St. Matthew. 1897.

Bennett, The Life of Christ according to St. Mark. 1907.

Broadus, The Gospel according to Mark. 1900.

Bruce, Gospel according to St. Mark. The Expositor's Greek Testament. 1897.

Burkitt, The Earliest Sources for the Life of Jesus. 1910.

Chadwick, The Gospel of Mark. The Expositor's Bible. 1887.

Clarke, The Gospel of Mark. American Commentary. 1881.

Du Boisson, The Origin and Characteristics of Mark. 1906.

Goguel, L'évangile de Marc et ses rapports avec ceux de Matthieu et de Luc. 1909.

Hoffmann, Das Marcusevangelium und seine Quellen. 1904.

Holtzmann, Die Synoptiker. Hand-Commentar. 1901.

Hunter, John Mark or the Making of a Saint. 1917.

Jacobus, The Gospel according to Mark. The Bible for Home and School. 1915.

Klostermann, Marcus. Lietzmann's Handbuch zum Neuen Testament. 1907.

Lagrange, Évangile selon St. Marc. 1911.

Lindsay, Mark's Gospel. T. & T. Clark's Handbooks. 1883.

Luckock, Footprints of the Son of Man as Traced by St. Mark. 1889.

Maclear, The Gospel of St. Mark. Cambridge Bible for Schools and Colleges. 1893.

Menzies, The Earliest Gospel: A Historical Study of the Gospel according to St. Mark. 1901.

Morison, Practical Commentary on the Gospel according to St. Mark. 7th edition. 1894.

Plummer, The Gospel according to St. Mark. Cambridge Greek Testament. 1915.

Plummer, The Gospel according to St. Mark. Cambridge Bible for Schools and Colleges. 1915.

Salmond, The Gospel according to St. Mark. New Century Bible.

Swete, The Gospel according to St. Mark. Second edition. 1902.

Taylor, The Gospel according to St. Mark. S. B. Convention Series.

Weiss, B., Das Marcusevangelium. Meyer-Kommentar. 1901.

Weiss, B., Die Geschichtlichkeit des Marcusevangeliums. 1905.

Weiss, B., Das Marcusevangelium und seine synoptischen Parallelen. 1872.

Weiss, J., Das älteste Evangelium. 1903.

Wellhausen, Das Evangelium Marci. Second edition. 1909.

Wendling, Urmarkus. 1905.

Wendling, Die Entstehung des Marcusevangeliums. 1908.

Wohlenberg, Das Evangelium des Marcus. Zahn Kommentar. 1910.